Claretta T. Pam

Massachusetts
Real Estate Salesperson

An exam preparation course

Book I

Massachusetts Real Estate Salesperson: An exam preparation course

Book I

Claretta T. Pam

Double Click Press

An Imprint of Innovative Publishers Inc.

Help Us Keep This Guide Up to Date

Every effort has been made by the author and editors to make this guide as accurate and useful as possible. However, many changes can occur after a guide is published.

We would like to hear from you concerning your experiences with this guide and how you feel it could be improved and be kept up to date. While we may not be able to respond to all comments and suggestions, we'll take all correspondence to heart and make certain to share them with the author. Please send your comments and suggestions to the following address:

Innovative Publishers Inc.
Double Click Press
Book ID #4745697
PO Box 170021
Boston, MA 02117

or you may email us at corrections@innovative-publishers.com

Cover art and design provided by
Taylor Pam – Fine Art LLC

Art available for purchase at
http://taylorpam.artistwebsites.com/featured/cos-116-taylor-pam.html

Innovative Publishers, Inc. & Double Click Press and colophon are trademarks of Open Nebula LLC, Intellectual Property Series.

Published and printed in the United States by
Innovative Publishers, Inc., Boston, Massachusetts

Innovative Publishers

Double Click Press

ISBN-13: 978-1-884711-85-5 Paperback

ISBN-13: 978-1-884711-16-9 Kindle

ISBN-13: 978-1-884711-17-6 AudioBook

Library of Congress Cataloging-in-Publication Data

Pam, Claretta T., 1969-
 Massachusetts real estate salesperson : an exam preparation course. Book I /
Claretta T. Pam. -- First edition.
     pages cm
  ISBN 978-1-884711-85-5 (pbk. : alk. paper) -- ISBN 978-1-884711-16-9 (ebook) --
ISBN 978-1-884711-17-6 (audiobook)
  1. Real estate agents--Massachusetts--Examinations, questions, etc. 2. Real
estate business--Massachusetts--Examinations, questions, etc. I. Title.
  HD278.P36 2014
  333.33076--dc23
                        2014031403

                 10 9 8 7 6 5 4 3 2 1   15 16 17 18

First edition. June 2015

For general information on our other products and services or for technical support, please contact our technical support within the United States at admin@innovative-publishers.com online at http://innovative-publishers.com.

Massachusetts Real Estate Salesperson: An exam preparation course Book I

Real Estate Learning Series

TABLE OF CONTENTS

CHAPTER 2

CONDOMINIUMS/COOPERATIVES/TIME SHARING/

LAND USE – SUBDIVISION

ACKNOWLEDGMENTS

To my children and grandchildren who continue to be my motivation and inspiration.

CHAPTER 1

KEY TERMS

Real property	Personal property	Property rights
Bundle of rights	annexation	Eminent domain
Police powers	zoning	Taxation
escheat	deed	Foreclosure
riparian	Dower and curtesy	encumbrances

CHAPTER 1 LEARNING OBJECTIVES

Upon your completion of this chapter you should be able to know the following:

1. What are fixtures, intent of parties and method of annexation
2. The differentiation between Tangible and Intangible property
3. What constitutes Corporeal and Incorporeal property
4. Bundle of Rights - what it means?
5. The concepts of Control, Possession, Enjoyment and Disposition of real property.
6. Rights of the Government
7. Tax on real estate and personal property and
8. Escheat
9. The difference between Freehold and Non-Freehold property
10. The different types of Freehold property and their significance
11. What is Concurrent Estate, its different types and their significance
12. What is a deed, types of deeds and deed validation requirements
13. What is a Will or Inheritance and conditions for its execution
14. The Law of Adverse Possession and its applicability
15. The key aspects of Eminent Domain law
16. What Escheat means?
17. The finer and deeper nuances of Foreclosure
18. What is an Easement?
19. Different types of Easements
20. What is a License?
21. What are dower and curtesy rights
22. What is tenancy as per dower rights
23. The clear differences between Riparian and Littoral rights and their significance under Massachusetts laws

PROPERTY/PROPERTY RIGHTS/OWNERSHIP

REAL VS PERSONAL PROPERTY

On reading this section completely, you will understand;

- What are fixtures, intent of parties and method of annexation
- The differentiation between Tangible and Intangible property
- What constitutes Corporeal and Incorporeal property

LAND

Land has economic and physical characteristics that allow individuals to create wealth.

The economic characteristics include the DUST principles. (Discussed in Chapter 6)

D - demand

U - utility

S - scarcity

T – transferability

Land can be composed of solid and immovable material of the earth. Though land is thought of as simply the surface material that one sees, it includes soil, rocks, minerals and things permanently attached by nature and plants.

There are three characteristics of land: No two parcels are exactly alike, the land is permanent and immovable.

Non-homogeneity – no two parcels are exactly alike. In real estate transactions, a seller could not simply substitute one property for another.

Immobility – While the dirt and natural material may be moved from place to place, the geographic location is fixed. One can not move 123 Main Street in Boston, MA to 456 North Street in Worcester, MA.

Permanency – Land is durable and largely indestructible. The elements of the land will remain the same regardless of natural or man made disasters.

REAL ESTATE
Real estate s land and manmade improvement permanently affixed to the land.

FIXTURES

A fixture is defined as an article in the form of personal property, which is annexed to the real estate in such a way that it is considered a fundamental part of the property. The article has to be physically annexed to the property or some such thing appurtenant thereto, for it to be regarded as a fixture. In other words, "a fixture is that which is permanently fastened or affixed to something, as an accessory and is unmovable".

The real property is regarded as affixed to a real estate when it is fastened to its roots, embedded within it, resting on it permanently or is perpetually attached to something that is eternal, such as through the use of cement, plaster, nuts, screws, nails or bolts.

Fixtures are the goods that have become an integral part of a particular real property to such an extent that an interest is created in them under real property laws. For example, a furnace installed in a house or building, a fire alarm and sprinkler system installed in a building or counters attached permanently to the flooring in a store.

Fixtures have attributes that are representative of both, real and personal property.

Trade fixtures

Trade fixtures can be personal property that is necessary to carry on a business. Even though items can be affixed to the property, the tenant may remove these items. Items not removed in a timely fashion may be considered abandoned. These items become the property of the landlord by accession.

intent of the parties

The attached object should be adapted for the intended purpose or use of the real estate such that it is essentially deemed inseparable from the property itself.

The intention of the individual attaching the object establishes the nature of the object as a 'fixture' or otherwise. The person concerned may not verbalize the intent; however, the courts will examine such expressions. The courts regard the tenant's intent, which is inferred after examining all the facts and situations related to the actual annexation of the article, such as the nature of the object attached, the method of annexation, the magnitude of integration of the object into the property and other factual information.

method of annexation (affixation)

Fixtures are generally annexed to rented premises for the benefit of the tenant without any aim of enhancing the value of the property. The landlord and the tenant may enter into an agreement with respect to the nature of an object to be used with the premises. Laws convene such a right in Massachusetts (M.G.L. c. 186) and such agreements are enforceable in circumstances where the rights of third persons are not infringed.

Often, the terms of a lease expressly define the respective rights of a landlord and the tenant concerning fixtures. If the lease explicitly specifies that the tenant reserves the right to remove particular objects, the fact that the rented premises could get damaged in the process is rendered irrelevant.

In situations where no agreement is entered into between the parties concerned, the objects attached by the tenant are allowed to be detached by the tenant, within the term of the tenancy, as long as such acts will not cause any damage to the premises.

The law is in favor of the tenant that specific objects may be considered as personal property instead of being treated as a part of the real estate. Such improvements are generally effected on the rented premises by the tenant for the purpose of personal convenience and use and hence must be treated as personal property.

The process of determining what goods are categorized as fixtures is governed by the common law rules between landlords and tenants (M.G.L. c. 184, § 12).

Fixtures annexed to a freehold property by a life tenant or his assigns are allowed to be removed during the tenure of the life estate or soon thereafter, within a judicious time period. (M.G.L.c. 184, § 12). The land owner reserves the right to removal of fixtures by making provision through a will or other instrument.

TANGIBLE AND INTANGIBLE

Tangible (corporeal) property is all personal property, apart from real property, which is inclusive of, but not limited to business equipment, furniture, office machinery, inventory and fixtures. In other words, tangible property is all physical property that has a definite form or structure such as dentist's drills, doctor's waiting room furnishings, and barbershop chairs etc.

Intangible property denotes any personal property, including elements in process, excluding accounts, chattel paper, documents, instruments, money, goods, investment property, stock, bonds, deposit accounts, letters of credit, letter-of-credit rights, commercial tort claims and oil, gas or various minerals prior to extraction.

CORPOREAL AND INCORPOREAL

Any real estate or personal property that has a tangible form and shape is termed as corporeal property. For example, building, vehicle and equipment etc.

Corporeal (tangible) property is comprised fully of substantial objects of a permanent nature, all of which may be interpreted under the general value of land. Some chattels exist that are annexed to the inheritance in such a manner that they are regarded as part of it and are referred to as *heirlooms*. Money provisioned or agreed to be invested in land is known as real estate.

Corporeal ownership refers to the ownership of tangible assets like land, building and money etc.

Any property that is intangible (does not have a tangible form and shape) and intellectual in nature is termed as incorporeal property. For example, copyrighted work, patents, lease or mortgage etc.

Incorporeal (intangible) property comprises of specific inheritable rights that are distinctly and strictly not corporeal in nature and not categorized as land, though by their own characteristics and through use, they are affixed to corporeal inheritances and are actually rights arising from them or concerning them.

Incorporeal property can be divided into two types;

     I.   Encumbrances – concerning material or immaterial things. E.g. leases, servitudes etc.

    II.   Full ownership – concerning something that is immaterial. E.g. patents, copyrights etc.

The commissioners appointed for partitioning incorporeal hereditaments involving multiple or joint tenants shall determine the best method for distributing the respective shares to the various parties concerned. The court will then make a decree to such effect. Any of the joint owners may request a sale and the court will order a sale, provided it is feasible.

The United States laws do not include hereditaments such as, advowsons, tithes, nor dignities, as inheritances.

Personal property may be derived from real property by severance. A tree on your property is real property. When it is cut down, it becomes personal property. Look from the tree can be used to construct the house. It is not real property. Real property is transferred by deed. Personal property is transferred by Bill of sale.

PROPERTY RIGHTS

On reading this section completely, you will understand;

- Bundle of Rights – what it means?
- The concepts of Control, Possession, Enjoyment and Disposition of real property.
- Where do these concepts apply?

BUNDLE OF RIGHTS

Bundle of Rights is a concept that is used to describe all the rights that a property owner possesses with respect to the property owned.

In other words, real estate ownership involves a complex set of rights and those rights have been traditionally assigned using a concept known as "Bundle of Rights". When a person buys a piece of land, he or she does not necessarily acquire all the rights to the property. The rights can be fragmented and disbursed to different parties.

The bundle of rights is a set of legal rights that are bestowed upon the real estate title holder. The bundle of rights includes;

- ✓ Right of Possession – the title holder owns the property
- ✓ Right of Control – the owner controls the use of the property
- ✓ Right of Exclusion – the owner regulates access to the property
- ✓ Right of Enjoyment – the title holder has the right to property usage in any legal manner
- ✓ Right of Disposition – the title holder has the right to buy or sell the property

Ownership of land is a far more complex issue than merely acquiring all the rights associated with it. A bundle of rights can be imagined to be analogous to a bundle of sticks, where each stick denotes an individual right. Such a bundle can be separated and reassembled. Every property owner acquires and possesses a set of "sticks" linked directly to the land.

Control, Possession, Enjoyment, Disposition

The highest form of land ownership is "fee simple estate" (explained later in this chapter). It is the absolute right of possession, enjoyment, control and disposition (transfer, sale), unconstrained by any other type of interest of estate. It is of perpetual duration and only government limitations apply such as eminent domain, escheat, taxation and police power.

CONTROL

Real property control typically involves zoning, development regulation of real estate, subdivision control (M.G.L. c. 41 §§ 81K – 81GG) and city planning.

In the twentieth century, as the United States moved from a rural to an urban civilization, local governments gained control over the location of housing, industry and trade. Zoning regulations and creation of Master Plans became standard practices. Federal, state and local governments began to regulate growth and development, to varying degrees, through statutory law.

Majority of the controls and restrictions on real estate and property arise from the actions of private developers and government units. They take several forms such as easements, restrictive covenants, defeasible fees and equitable servitudes.

Easements are rights that allow the use of property of another person for specific purposes. An example of common easement is the permit to a telephone company to run its line through a private property. Restrictive Covenants refer to provisions in a deed restricting the use of property and prohibiting particular uses. They are similar to equitable servitudes, but run with the land as the restrictions are included within the deed. Land developers use these to define minimum house sizes, setback boundaries and aesthetic requirements for enhancing the neighborhood. Equitable Servitudes are restrictions on the use of property enforceable in an Equity court. These are created by using the language of the promise in the format of an agreement (Covenant) between two parties. The courts have merged equitable servitude and restrictive covenants into one single legal concept today. In defeasible fee estates, the grantee receives land from the grantor subject to specific conditions. For example a person may offer a land to another person with the condition that it be used for school purpose only. Defeasible fee restricts the possessor in the use of the property. Failure to observe this condition by the grantee will transfer the property back to the grantor.

Other laws related to property control are Planned Communities, Nuisance, Waste laws, Eminent Domain etc., some of which are discussed in detail in the following sections.

POSSESSION

Possession refers to the ownership, control or occupancy of land or personal property by an individual. The term 'possession' has various meanings and thus ambiguous in interpretation.

Consequently, possession or lack of it, is frequently the subject of dispute in civil lawsuits involving real and personal.

Although confusing, possession and ownership are two completely different concepts. It is often assumed that the person who possesses an object is most probably its owner. For example, people may say they own clothes, shoes etc. But the owner of an object may not necessarily possess an object. To avoid confusion, the word possession is often modified by adding another term describing it, such as actual, adverse, sole, superficial, legal, illegal, constructive, exclusive and physical etc. All these originate from the legal term 'actual possession'.

Actual possession is the most common interpretation, i.e. having physical custody of an object. However, sometimes the term possession in fact, is used to denote immediate physical contact. For example, carrying a wallet in your jacket pocket means you have actual possession it. But, by necessity, this is very limited. To deal with such situations, the courts have broadened the scope of possession.

Constructive possession is a legal concept created to extend possession to situations in which a person has no custody of an object.

Also known as "possession in law", constructive possession refers to a situation where a person has awareness and control of an object, but does not have physical contact with it. For example, a property leased out to a tenant by its owner. The owner is aware of and in control of the property, but does not actually reside on the property.

The concept of adverse possession is explained in detail this chapter.

ENJOYMENT

Under Massachusetts law, tenants possess the right to "quiet enjoyment" of their property, i.e. the right to reside in and enjoy the premises without any disturbance or interference from the landlord or neighbors. M.G.L. c.186 § 14 permits a tenant to sue the landlord and recover up to three months' rent or damages at actuals, higher of the two, in addition to reasonable attorney's charges in case the landlord breaches its covenant (promise) of providing quiet enjoyment.

A covenant, in general, is an agreement between two individuals or parties to do something or desist from doing it. The right to quiet enjoyment is included in the covenants related to real estate. Courts recognize quiet enjoyment covenant into each rental agreement or tenancy between the landlord and tenant.

Other rights concerning quiet enjoyment can be customized for specific situations and included in the tenancy agreement.

A person who owns a property in fee simple wields the right to possession, enjoyment, control and disposition of such real property. Disposition usually means the sale, exchange or loss of property, regardless of it being voluntary or involuntary.

In other words, it is the act of disposing i.e. the transfer of real property under the care or possession of a different person or the parting with, giving up of or alienation of property. The final settlement of a real property matter with reference to court decisions or judge's ruling is termed as disposition, irrespective of the resolution level.

LIMITS TO PROPERTY RIGHTS

On reading this section completely, you will understand;

- Rights of others (neighbors)
- Rights of the Government
- Tax on real estate and personal property and
- Escheat

RIGHTS OF OTHERS

In the early days, land was abundant and neighbors were far spread out. As population grew and urban areas expanded, so did property disputes between neighbors.

Adjoining landowners are those next-door and backyard neighbors owning lands, which share common boundaries and hence mutual rights, duties and responsibilities.

Landowners are expected to make decent use of their property without undue interference with the rights of owners of adjacent land. Any activity that a person does which misappropriates the adjacent land or infringes upon the enjoyment of the adjoining land by its owner is considered unlawful.

For example, a man purchases a home in a zoned residential area and transforms it into an office. He converts the backyard into a parking area but encroaches three feet beyond his property boundary into the adjoining land. This amounts to unlawful use of adjacent property in a number of ways. He has encroached on his neighbor's land and significantly interfered with his neighbor's right to enjoying his property. This man can be sued in a Tort Action for creating Nuisance and the neighbor could win damages and an injunction to halt unlawful use of his property. Further, this man has violated zoning laws through use of residential property for commercial activities without obtaining variance.

Property owners possess the right to change their land level or construct foundations or embankments so long as they take appropriate precautions such as constructing a retaining wall to prevent soil spills on adjoining land (M.G.L. c. 243).

Lateral Support

This is the right of a landowner to have his or her land in its natural condition, maintained in place from all the sides by neighboring land such that it will not subside. A land is considered to be in its natural condition if there are no buildings or structures constructed on it.

A landowner has the legal right to lateral support from an adjacent landowner, which is enforceable in the court of law. It is the duty of the landowner, who excavates close to the neighbor's boundary, to prevent any injury that may be caused by removal of lateral support to the neighbor's property. Since lateral support is deemed an absolute property right, an adjacent landowner is held responsible for damages to natural condition of the land irrespective of any act of negligence or otherwise.

If the landowner had constructed buildings on the land, the lateral support rights change. The building places additional weight on the land, enhancing the burden on lateral support. In such cases, the landowner can win damages for injuries caused to the building due to excavation only if the neighbor has displayed negligence. In some cases, landowners planning excavation are required to give notice to adjacent landowners so that they may take necessary precaution to protect their property. Adjacent landowners failing to take precautions do not absolve the excavator of any liability for negligence. If the excavator fails to notify adjacent landowners then this is treated as negligence by the courts and the excavator is held responsible for damages although the excavation itself may not have been performed negligently.

If proven through evidence that lateral support for a neighbor's land was removed by a landowner, the neighbor can claim damages for an amount equal to the cost of restoring the land to its value prior to removal of lateral support or to is former condition, least of the two. The neighbor may be granted an injunction for prohibiting the landowner from further excavation, if it is proven to pose clear danger to all adjacent lands and cause irreparable damage.

Subjacent Support

This is the absolute right of the landowner to have his or her land supported from beneath the surface. One person may own the surface of the land while another person may own the subjacent surface. The surface landowner has the right to have it maintained in its natural condition without sinking caused due to withdrawal of subjacent material by the subsurface owner. An adjacent landowner, who comes across a subterranean stream, during excavation, and causes the neighbor's land soil to sink or collapse is liable for any resulting injuries. The surface owner acquires the right to legal action against the subsurface owner for deprivation of subjacent support when the land actually collapses and not during excavation.

The construction of buildings on the land surface does not diminish a person's subjacent support rights, but changes the circumstances for claiming damages for withdrawal of subjacent support. In case of damage to such buildings the onus is on the owner to prove that support was removed negligently.

Encroachments

An encroachment is a trespass on the property of another person without that person's permission. No landowner has any legal right to construct buildings or erect structures such that any part, irrespective of size, protrudes beyond his property and intrudes on adjacent lands. An encroaching landowner is required to get rid of the roof space of a building that overhangs an adjacent plot. On their refusal the contiguous land owner may personally take away as much encroachment that deprives him or her of full enjoyment of his or her property, but in case of any negligence, he or she is liable for damages.

In case any expense was incurred for removal of encroachments from the adjacent plot, such expense can be claimed by the person whose property was encroached upon from the encroaching landowner. Such lawsuit can be filed under the theory of "nuisance" or theory of "trespass" to claim monetary damages or obtain an injunction against continuation of encroachment or enforce removal.

Light, Air and View

No landowner enjoys an absolute right over light and air from or traversing over adjacent land or to a view over adjacent property. Zoning laws applicable to localities may specify that any type of construction undertaken should not deprive an adjacent landowner of sufficient air, light and view. In the same way, restrictive covenants in deeds or easements impact a person's duty toward neighbor's right to air, light and view. Lack of zoning laws or agreements allow a person to erect structures on his or her own property with disregard to the fact that he or she may be depriving the adjacent neighbor of air, light and view that was enjoyed prior to construction of the building. An exception to this is a structure that blocks air, light and view with the sole aim of injuring a neighbor without providing any benefit or pleasure to the owner, e.g. a "spite" fence. The courts do not usually permit such structures.

Trees and Shrubs

Property owners must not allow trees or hedges on their property to infringe on the rights of adjacent plot owners. For example, if a person is aware that a tree on his or her property is decayed and likely to fall and damage the neighbor's property, then it is that person's duty to eliminate such danger. A tree existing on the boundary of contiguous plots belongs to both adjacent property owners. Each owner acquires an interest identical with the part growing on his or her plot. Each landowner can cut intruding tree branches or roots at the boundary of his or her property regardless of any injuries that may have been sustained through such intrusion, but taking adequate care to prevent killing the entire tree.

Water rights

Right to use the water that directly abuts the land, passes through the land or which lies above or beneath the land. Also called riparian rights, this topic will be covered in detail in later in this Chapter.

Riparian Land

Land bordering natural watercourse – lake, river, stream etc. is termed as Riparian land or zone. The owner of such land up to the water's edge is the Riparian owner and possesses Riparian rights. More detailed explanation is provided later in this Chapter.

Subsurface Rights

Subsurface refers to the area below the surface of land or water body. The land below the surface of the water is owned by the public, except in situations where a person owns land on both the sides of the water body. Similarly, land existing way below the surface of a real property, subsoil, carries certain rights that are vested with the local authorities such as the department of environment protection and others.

Mineral rights

The rights to minerals found generally in the subsurface (subsoil) are termed as Mineral Rights. Mineral resources are oil, gas, soil, sand, ores, fossil fuels, gravel, sulphur, metals, rock etc. found in coastal waters or land below the water level. The local authorities possess all such mineral rights and the surface land owners do not have any right to explore any such minerals without authorization from the concerned body who owns the mineral rights.

GOVERNMENT RIGHTS

Some government rights are exercised for the common good of the community.

Eminent Domain

The government is empowered to take private property for public use. This power is known as *eminent domain*. The power to take public property for public purposes arises from the US constitution, state constitutions, federal and state laws (M.G.L. c. 79). Local governments such as cities, towns and counties as well, possess the power of eminent domain.

For example, if the Massachusetts Highway Department requires a portion of a property for a public use, it is empowered to take the title of that property from its lawful owner by eminent domain.

(Repeated in Sections below, with greater details)

Police Power

The tenth amendment to the U.S. constitution bestows such powers, amongst others, upon the states, which they may delegate to their political subsections such as counties, towns, villages, cities or large boroughs, in order to devise measures to preserve and protect the interests, security, morals, health, safety and welfare of the general public. It is the basic right of the government to enact laws and regulations for the greater good of the communities. The government holds such power to apply judicious control over property and people. Under the U.S. system of governance, only states possess the right to devise laws in accordance with their police power. The federal government's lawmaking power is restricted to particular grants of power included in the U.S. Constitution.

If any law enacted on the basis of police power does not meet its primary objectives, then it amounts to unconstitutional deprivation of life, freedom and property. The most common hurdle to a law enacted on the basis of police power is that it involves a taking. A taking happens when the government deprives an individual of his or her property or directly intrudes upon or significantly disrupts the individuals use and enjoyment of such property. Police power permits the destruction or restriction of such property that proves to be threat to the general public, without the payment of any compensation. Further, it bestows the right upon the police to take action without a court hearing or such other process protections, as necessary, to protect the general public's welfare. Persons adversely affected may contest such actions by initiating habeas corpus proceedings and similar other post-restriction means. Certain states have restricted their police powers through legislation and the state's constitutional provisions.

In dealing with cases concerning the application of police power, the courts follow the doctrine of "balance of interests" to ascertain situations where the general public's right to good health and welfare may prevail over private or individual rights. These include imposing restrictions on the use of property (viz. zoning laws) or running a business.

Types of police power rights that are applicable to real property are;

> ➢ Housing codes
> ➢ Rent control
> ➢ Subdivision regulations
> ➢ Public Nuisance Ordinances
> ➢ Zoning
> ➢ Condemnation Proceedings
> ➢ Special Operating Licenses

Police power also forms the basis for enacting various substantive laws related to zoning, land use, building codes, fire, bicycles, automobiles, parking, crime, gambling, liquor, nuisances, discrimination, schools and sanitation etc. Police power does not specifically indicate the state government's right to form police forces, although that right is included within it.

Zoning and Building Codes

Zoning

Zoning means the division or segregation of a municipality into multiple districts; the regulation of land, building and structures within such districts on the basis of their construction, nature and use; and assigning such districts for specific uses for the welfare of the general public.

Zoning refers to the regulation of real property usage by the local government, restricting a particular area (or zone) to be used for residential, commercial and industrial or such other purposes. The local government initially reviews the nature of the property and its fitness for a specific use. It then enacts laws in line with a well-thought and detailed plan with the aim of preventing arbitrary exercise of vested powers. The purpose of the detailed plan is to regulate the use of real property in the whole municipality or in a significant part of it. Individual chunks of property are not permitted to be isolated for giving special treatment. For example, one or more portions of property cannot be treated as a separate zone and subjected to restrictions that are not applicable to similar adjoining pieces of land.

Zoning laws usually restrict dimensions in every zone. Most laws mandate specific building features and restrict the number and location of loading and parking areas as well as use of hoardings and signs. Some other laws involve creation of space for schools, parks and such other public utilities.

Zoning helps city and town planners to achieve organized change and growth; control population density; create attractive and healthy residential areas; besides assuring property owners and residents about the stability of surrounding areas. Zoning requires careful thought for future growth and development, population density, provision of sufficient drainage and storm sewers, pedestrian walkways, streets and such other factors.

Massachusetts zoning laws (M.G.L. c. 40A) bestows power on towns and cities to adopt ordinances and byelaws for controlling the use of land and buildings.

Massachusetts laws on regional planning (M.G.L. c. 40B) allow a city or town to team up with other cities or towns to devise a plan for promoting development and prosperity in their jurisdiction. Particularly, M.G.L. c. 40B, § § 20 – 23, relate to affordable housing. Chapter 40B is also called by the names, "Anti-Snob Zoning Act" as well as "Comprehensive Permit Statute".

Massachusetts smart-growth zoning laws (M.G.L. c. 40R) encourage "smart growth" with the aim of preserving open spaces and simultaneously giving a boost to affordable housing.

Building Codes

Building Codes are a series of ordinances legislated by a state or local government body, setting minimum requirements that have to be achieved in the construction and maintenance of structures. A building code generally comprises multiple documents that specify the minimum requirements with respect to various aspects of construction such as gas, electricity, plumbing, mechanics, fire-alarm systems etc. Building codes usually govern all the aspects of construction including structural design, building materials, conservation measures, environmental control, light, ventilation, sanitation facilities and fire prevention.

State and local government bodies are empowered to decree building codes as a subset of their police powers, in accordance with the Tenth Amendment of the Federal Constitution. The first National Building Code was formulated in 1905 by the National Board of Fire Examiners. Over the decades the building codes evolved significantly until the 1990s when the National Building Code was re-established by the American Insurance Association (AIA).

Since then most of the states have created laws stipulating construction standards. These laws were enacted by the states in order to establish uniformity in building regulations and to ensure that the citizens in the state received equal protection from building laws. Usually, the state government enacts building construction laws at a general level, while the local governments devise specific regulations applicable to their jurisdiction.

In Massachusetts, the Board of Building Regulations and Standards (BBRS) creates laws and governs all activity pertaining to building construction. It derives its power and authority from Massachusetts General Laws (M.G.L. c. 143 §§ 93 – 100) to adopt legislations, administer state building code provisions and conduct different construction related programs.

Building codes, that regulate the safety and construction standards of building, exist in parallel with the zoning ordinances and do not contradict them. Both co-exist on the platform of police power; building codes ensure minimum standards and safety of buildings and structures; and zoning stabilizes real property use. Zoning laws are relatively more permanent in nature, while building codes are more flexible and are subject to changes with technological advancement.

See building code related laws in the appendix.

TAXATION

Property Tax

A property tax (also known as millage tax) is a type of levy on a property which is required to be paid by the property owner. This tax is usually levied by the governing authority of the region, within which the property is situated, such as the national government, state, county, municipality or geographical region. Different jurisdictions can subject the same property to the same tax. There are four main types of property;

- ➢ Land
- ➢ Improvements to Land (immovable man-made structures e.g. buildings)
- ➢ Personal Property (movable objects)
- ➢ Intangible Property

Real property (or real estate or realty) denotes the combination of land and any improvements to it. The property tax system empowers the government to conduct an appraisal of each property to assess its monetary value and determine the tax proportionately. Real property is taxed at different rates depending on its classification into categories such as residential, industrial, commercial etc.

United States Taxation

In the United States, for most local governments, property tax is the prime source of revenue. This tax is applicable on real estate as well as personal property. It is mostly always calculated as a fair market value multiplied by an assessment ratio multiplied by a tax rate. Values are established by local officials and open to dispute by property owners. A significant advantage of property tax is that it always generates the required revenue from tax levies for municipalities.

The property tax is normally administered by the local government. Many states impose restrictions on local jurisdictions on the manner of taxing properties. Since most properties are subjected to multiple taxes by different local jurisdictions, many states have made provisions for uniform tax values among such jurisdictions.

State Estate or Death Tax: Estate Pays

Many states impose taxes on real estate owners (decedents) as well as on the decedent's personal property within the state. A single tax rate could become applicable to all assets included in the estate or the rate could vary on the basis of the recipient and the portion of property inherited. For example, a state may levy a lower tax rate on property inherited by a child as compared to that inherited by a distant cousin of the deceased. It may be noted that in a few states, the estate tax system is in the process of being phased out.

State Inheritance Tax: Property Recipient Pays

In states where inheritance tax laws apply, taxes are required to be paid by the person receiving the inherited property (in contrast to estate taxes paid from decedent's estate). Inheritance tax rates and exemptions could be different depending on the recipient of the property. For example, the decedent's spouse may incur a lower tax rate than the decedent's friend. In many states the inheritance tax system is being phased out.

"Pickup" Tax

Despite having estate or inheritance tax laws, many states practice the "pickup" tax system with respect to the decedent's death. According to this tax system, although a state tax return is required to be filed by the estate (or by the recipient inheriting the property), the state obtains its share from the tax that the estate is currently paying the IRS. This means, in many states no additional tax is required to be paid besides the amount already being deposited with the federal government.

Massachusetts Taxation

In Massachusetts too, property tax is a prime source of revenue for the local governments. The legislature has empowered the local governments to administer the property tax system under supervision of the state and determine the property tax rates locally. In 1980, a law known as "Proposition $2^{1}/_{2}$" was passed through popular ballot, which establishes limits on property and other tax rates. Such limit calculation on property tax has three key sections as follows;

1. Levy Ceiling

In any one year, a community is not allowed to collect taxes exceeding 2.5% of the total full and fair cash value considering all the taxable real and personal property existing in the community.

2. Levy Increase Limit

The increase in the tax amount collected annually should not exceed 2.5% over that of the previous year, combined with the amount gained through increased property values.

3. New Growth

The state department of revenue (DOR), every year, computes a "new growth" amount for each municipality, permitting that community to enhance its levy a specific amount over the 2.5% ceiling to provision for value-additions in the local properties such as high-priced homes to subdivision of farms.

A municipality is allowed, but not mandated, to collect taxes up to the levy limit. It can collect less than the limit as well. If it wishes to raise more money than permitted under the ceiling or increase limit, it has to obtain approval of the voters for an "override" or "debt exclusion" of Proposition $2^1/_2$, with the exception of water and sewer debt. Tax increases achieved through debt exclusion have to be associated with a specific cost and have to expire at a later date; while those achieved through override establish a new benchmark for all the 2.5% increases in the future.

Tax Exemptions and Abatements

Some municipalities allow state-authorized exemptions on property tax of up to 30% for low-price, owner-occupied properties. Tax exemptions and abatements concerning real estate are deductions from the property tax amount that property owners are required to pay to the city or town of their residence. Exemptions and abatements can be applicable to the entire or part of the total property taxes payable.

In Massachusetts, the cities and towns are allowed to provide real estate tax exemptions to surviving spouses and minor children, seniors, the blind, property-owners facing hardships and specific disabled veterans fulfilling financial residency and other required eligibility criteria. Cities and towns conducting property tax work-off programs may provide abatement to senior volunteers fulfilling eligibility criteria.

The benefits vary across cities and towns and there are income and asset limits defined for eligibility purpose.

ESCHEAT

Under Massachusetts law, if a person dies intestate and has no known legal heirs then the property of the deceased transfers (escheats) to the state. In several other states, such property generally transfers to the county. Thereafter, the Commonwealth has complete power to either retain or dispose it off. This concept of escheat has its roots in the English law which believes that truly orphaned real property could be harmful to public interests.

ESTATES

On reading this section completely, you will understand;

- The difference between Freehold and Non-Freehold property
- The different types of Freehold property and their significance
- What is Concurrent Estate, its different types and their significance

FREEHOLD VS NON-FREEHOLD

Freehold and Non-Freehold (a.k.a. Leasehold), both, are types of property that are developed according to the common law system. Freehold estates can be held forever or until the possessor is alive. Non-Freehold or Leasehold estates can be held for a fixed time period as per the calendar. Although, freehold and non-freehold property are differentiated by the time duration of their respective possession, both are deemed as present possessory estates.

A freehold estate means a right of title to land that is categorized into two key elements; Immobility – indicating that the property concerned is either land or simply an interest attached to or derived from it, and Indeterminate Duration – denotes that the ownership duration is not fixed. Freehold estates are of three main types – fee simple (Absolute, Determinable and Upon Condition), fee tail and life estate.

Non-Freehold estates are typically interests in real property that do not involve ownership and are not inheritable. Non-Freehold estates are of four main types – estate for years, tenancy from year to year, tenancy at will and tenancy at sufferance.

Fee Simple Absolute

This is the most extensive interest in real property that a person can possess, as it is restricted completely to the person and his or her assigns permanently, and it does not attract any limitations or special conditions

For example, a person might buy a plot of land and its deed may specify that the grantor transfers his or her property "to grantee and his or her heirs". This lawfully creates a fee simple absolute. The grantee gets the right to possess the land immediately and solely and deal with it in any way as desired such as remove trees, grow crops, build structures on it, sell it or dispose through a will. This type of estate is regarded as perpetual. On the owner's death, if such estate's distribution was not provisioned, it is inherited inevitably by the owner's heirs.

Fee Simple Determinable

Also known as base fee or qualified fee, a fee simple determinable continues until a specific event occurs. On occurrence of such an event, the estate automatically terminates through operation of law and the ownership regresses to the grantor or their heirs.

For example, if the grantor specified in the conveyance, "to grantee and his or her heirs as long as (so long as) utilized for purposes of education". Here the grantor's intent is explicitly stated at the time of creating the estate. As and when the grantee desists from using the estate for purposes related to education, the grantor gets the right to immediate possession. The grantee's estate is limited to the time period during which the property is used for education related activities only.

The grantor's interest is called *possibility of reverter*.

Fee Upon Condition

This type of estate is one that terminates when the power of termination or the right of re-entry is exercised after a specific condition is violated. A fee simple determinable estate expires automatically through operation of law, as soon as a specified event occurs. In comparison, this type of estate continues to hold even after the particular event occurs, until the grantor exercises their power to terminate, in order to end it or divest it.

For example, the grantor conveys land through a condition as, "to the grantee or his or her heirs, but in case the premises are utilized for commercial purposes barring the sale of furniture, the grantor reserves the right to re-enter and re-possess the property".

The grantor holds the power to terminate the grantee's fee by re-entry into the premises on violation of the specified condition. However, re-entry is completely at the discretion of the grantor. The grantee's estate continues up to the time that the grantor chooses to either enter the premises or resorts to some action in order to recover possession. When the grantor actually re-enters the premises, the residual portion of the grantee's estate gets forfeited.

Fee Tail

This type of freehold estate potentially lasts forever. The fee tail originated in feudal England as a method of retaining properties within families to the maximum extent possible. Although a fee tail may potentially continue for an infinite time period, it may cease in situations where the first fee tail tenant is unable to create a lineal descendent.

A fee tail (M.G.L. c. 184) is a freehold estate that permits family land to be passed on to subsequent generations by restraining inheritance to the lineal descendants of the property owner. It prohibits disposition of real property through sale, bequeathing through Will or alienation and results in the real estate being passed on automatically to the property owner's legal heirs on his or her death. The original purpose of fee tail was to retain family estates within the succession line and preventing illegal offspring from inheriting them. Typically, the possession of such real estate is passed on from eldest son to eldest son so long as the bloodline progresses. If the tenant in tail dies without any lineal descendants, then the fee tail is subjected to reversion or remainder.

Fee tail has been abolished everywhere in the United States, except in the four states – Massachusetts, Maine, Delaware and Rhode Island. In Massachusetts, like in Maine and Delaware, fee tail can be sold or passed on through a deed like any other real property. In these states, fee tail only impacts property transfer through a Will.

Life Estate (Remainder)

A Life Estate is a freehold estate that ends on the death of the possessor of the property (the life tenant). Under property law, the intent to establish a life estate is proven when the grantor states, "to X for life". The person granted (the grantee) a life estate is known as the *life tenant*. On death of the life estate tenant, the life estate "reverts" (are transferred back) to their original owner or their heirs (**the remaindermen**). For example, if you own a house, you may sell or hand over your house to your offspring, but retain a "life estate", thus reserving the right to reside, use, enjoy and manage the house till your death. Here, your offspring are known as the **"remaindermen"**.

A life estate is usually formed through a deed by conveying the property to the remainderman; however, it may also be formed through a lease. Life estates are frequently granted through Wills. The formation of a life estate does not require any special language as long as the grantor's intent to form such an estate is evident. The "remainder interest", which means the property ownership in favor of the remainderman, comes into effect immediately on the death of the life tenant.

The life tenant holds the right to use and possess the property during his or her lifetime, including the rights to accrued rents and profits, besides being responsible to bear the costs of maintaining the property. However, the life tenant is not permitted to sell or waste the property without seeking the consent of the remaindermen.

A life estate is non-inheritable and is limited to the life of the grantee (life tenant) or *per autre vie* (to the life of another).

Benefits of a Life Estate

1. A life tenant enjoys the right to reside in their house during their lifetime, until death. A life estate provides security to the life tenant in their home. In case the house is transferred outright to a new owner, then such a new owner may immediately sell off the house and evict the previous owner from the premises.

2. A life estate enables you to pass on your house to your offspring or other relatives without undergoing a probate. On the death of the life tenant, the property immediately transfers to the remaindermen without any need for a probate proceeding, thus saving valuable time, money and effort for the family.

   For example, if the title of your own house is in your name alone at the time of your death, it cannot be transferred to your heirs unless it goes through probate. Creating a Will does not help prevent a probate as the Will merely indicates to the court, how the property in your estate is to be distributed.

3. Creating a life estate helps achieve eligibility for MassHealth / Medicaid and protects your house from liens and estate recovery by MassHealth / Medicaid. Life estates are often leveraged for preserving the house for the purpose of long-term care planning. If the details required by MassHealth rules are not provided, then such transfers trigger the waiting period of five years in order to become eligible. Following the transfer period of five years, the property has to be protected. However, the property may be subjected to a lien, but only amounting to the life estate's value and not the entire property's value.

4.   Retaining a life estate in your house means that it continues to be treated as an asset of your estate for the purposes of estate tax and enables your children to benefit from "step up in basis" of the real property. Thus when your children inherit the property it is valued as per the date of death and not as per the date of acquisition of the property by you. This helps your children to avoid capital gains tax when they sell the property, unless the property appreciates to a value higher than on the date of death before the sale.

5.   Life estate ownership is established merely recording a new deed signed by the current property owners. The costs involved are reasonable. If a copy of the present deed is not available, it may be obtained from the Registry of Deeds for a small fee. You may order a title search to confirm the present precise ownership of the property.

6.   A death certificate for every individual lifetime owner has to be recorded with the Registry of Deeds, along with a simple affidavit declaring that deceased Lifetime Owner was not in possession of any assets valued higher than the Estate Tax limit (From January 1, 2012, Federal Estate Tax is applicable on gross estates whose value equals or exceeds $ 5.0 million. Under Massachusetts law, Estate Tax becomes applicable on estates whose value equals or exceeds $1.0 million). This is usually done upon death of the life tenant, to clear the title to the owned real estate in the form for Life Estate Ownership. This is a simple and economical method of title clearance that can be completed immediately following the last Life Tenant Owner's death, or any time before the sale of the real estate, as convenient. If the real estate was not owned in the form for Life Estate Ownership, then it has to undergo the probate process and the title would be cleared only after the probate process is completed.

7.   If the Life Tenant Owner, at the time of death, owned assets worth a value where estate tax becomes applicable, then the estate tax will have to be paid and an estate tax return filed before clearance of the title to the real estate. Estate taxes will have to be paid and returns will have to be filed, irrespective of whether the real estate was owned in the Life Estate Ownership form or otherwise.

NON FREEHOLD

Non Freehold is also referred to as leasehold. It includes estate for years, estate year to year, tenancy at will and tenancy at sufferance. Non freehold estates are created by giving possession of or the use of real estate without title. The giving of possession may be in writing (lease) or oral (sometimes referred to as tenancy at will).

The following terms are used interchangeably:

Landlord/Lessor

Tenant/Lessee

Estate for years

This estate or tenancy is created by lease (contract) in which the landlord (lessor) grants to the tenant (lessee) the right to use the real estate for a specific period of time. An agreed upon amount of rent is clearly stipulated. The lease is subject to specific conditions (covenants). The lease may be for a period ranging from one day to ninety-nine years and the tenant must surrender possession to the landlord at the expiration of the lease.

Estate year to year

Estate year to year is also referred to as periodic tenancy. This tenancy has definite payment intervals and extends year to year no matter how frequently the rent is paid (i.e. monthly, quarterly, or semi-annually). Either landlord or tenant must give one year's notice in order to terminate the lease.

Tenancy at will (M.G.L.c. 186, § 13)

Tenancy at will is created orally or by lease for an agreed upon amount of rent and without a specific amount of time. A tenancy may be created at such time as the landlord accepts rent and gives the tenant access (key or code) to the apartment or dwelling. The tenancy may be terminated by 1)legal notice from each party (in Massachusetts, the minimum notice required is thirty (30) days; or 2) death of the tenant. The tenancy will not be terminated by death of the landlord.

Tenancy at Sufferance (M.G.L. c. 186, § 3)

Tenancy at sufferance is created when a tenant remains in possession of a property after the tenancy has been legally terminated. The landlord may recover payments for use of the property while in sufferance. Note: If the landlord accepts any payment before the tenant in sufferance leaves, a tenancy at will is now created.

> *Hold over tenant* – while similar to tenancy at sufferance, a hold over tenant is one whose lease has expired and they remain in possession of the property. They have the same rights as a tenant at sufferance.

CONCURRENT ESTATES

Concurrent Estate, also known as Co-ownership, is the simultaneous ownership of an exclusive interest in a particular real property by more than one person or entity. When different types of trusts, partnerships or corporate entities becomes owners in a concurrent estate or in severalty, such entities are viewed leniently as a variant of co-ownership between the partners, stockholders, members or beneficiaries.

Under Massachusetts law (M.G.L.c. 184, § 7), only three types of concurrent estates are recognized, as below;

> ➤ Tenancy-by-the-Entirety

> ➤ Joint Tenancy

> ➤ Tenancy-in-Common

Tenancy by the Entirety

A tenancy-by-the-entirety is a method of co-ownership, applicable only to married couples as long as they are legally married. According to a very old common law, spouses are treated as one person in situations concerning property ownership. Although most of the states have abolished this practice of co-ownership, Massachusetts law still recognizes it and holds it valid. As tenants by the entirety, the spouses enjoy exactly similar right of survivorship as intrinsic to joint tenancy. Some of the limitations of tenancy-by-the-entirety are;

> ➤ While their status is legally married, neither the husband nor the wife possesses an interest individually or separately, that is permitted to be sold, mortgaged or leased

> ➤ The spouses are not allowed to break up or partition their property

> ➤ Neither spouse is permitted to convey his or her share without the signature of the other

> ➤ Neither spouse can create a will to bequeath any interest to a third party

> ➤ In the event of a divorce, the tenancy-by-the-entirety gets converted by default into a tenancy-in-common with each partner getting one-half ownership interest in the property

> ➤ The termination of tenancy-by-the-entirety is considered valid only when both the spouses together convey the property, or in case of a divorce or death

> ➤ In case, a debtor spouse dies before the non-debtor spouse, the right of survivorship removes all lien applicable to the debtor spouse, thus precluding any claims on the property by any third party

Massachusetts law stipulates that the deed must include clear proof that the title is related to tenancy-by-the-entirety and not to tenancy-in-common. If the deed simply implies the right of survivorship, then it will most likely be interpreted as a joint tenancy and not tenancy-by-the-entirety. The words on a conveyance deed that may be acceptable could read as "grand A and B, a legally married couple, as tenants-by-the-entirety". If land is conveyed to two persons, who are not spouses of each other, as tenants by the entirety then an estate in joint tenancy will be created and not a tenancy-in-common.

One important advantage that differentiates tenancy-by-the-entirety from joint tenancy is linked to the prime residence of the married couple. In a tenancy-by-the- entirety the individual spouses hold an exclusive 100 percent right to the principal residence. If a married couple is in a joint tenancy, then each joint tenant holds an unbroken 50 percent right to the property. The joint tenancy permits 50 percent of the property of either spouse to be subjected to lien by a creditor, if such a situation arises. The precise impact of tenancy-by-the-entirety is that one spouse's creditor is not allowed to compel the sale of the property since the other non-creditor spouse has 100 percent ownership in the property. However, the law (M.G.L.c. 209, § 1) provisions that both the spouses will always be jointly or severally liable for any debts due to lends provided to any individual spouse or family member.

According to some recent decisions by Massachusetts courts, transferring a title into tenancy-by-the-entirety following a judgment lien against one spouse but prior to the sale of the property prohibits the creditor from selling the property. If the death of the debtor spouse precedes that of the non-debtor spouse, all liens against the debtor spouse are erased due to right of survivorship, releasing the property from all such claims.

According to the M.G.L.c. 209, §§ 1, 2, 6, the real and personal property belonging to any person continues to be treated as the separate property of the respective spouse post-marriage too.

Joint Tenancy

According to Massachusetts law, when the parties acquiring title choose co-ownership in joint tenancy, their deed must obviously classify the joint tenancy. For example, "grantees will accept title as joint tenants and the survivor amongst them". A more compliant way is "grantees will accept title as joint tenants along with right of survivorship". If right of survivorship is explicitly expressed, then it will not be considered as tenancy-in-common as there is not right of survivorship in tenancy-in-common.

Similar to most other states, Massachusetts decrees the existence of the four unities;

> ➤ Possession – all the joint tenants enjoy entire possession

> ➤ Interest – all the joint tenants have identical ownership interests

> ➤ Time – all the joint tenants obtain their interests simultaneously

> ➤ Title – all the joint tenants secured their ownership interests through a single title document

Tenancy in Common

Massachusetts law always treats the concurrent estate to be tenancy-in-common, if the entire interests in property are transferred to more than one person or entity, unless the specific wordings of the deed indicate otherwise. Tenants in common could have different percentage share of ownership.

TRANSFER OF RIGHTS

On reading this section completely, you will understand;

- What is a deed, types of deeds and deed validation requirements
- What is a Will or Inheritance and conditions for its execution
- The Law of Adverse Possession and its applicability
- The key aspects of Eminent Domain law
- What Escheat means
- The finer and deeper nuances of Foreclosure

DEED

Real estate transactions in Massachusetts commonly involve two types of deeds. Conveyance has been traditionally decreed through a *Warranty Deed* in the western part of the state and *Quitclaim* Deed is widely used in the eastern part.

Warranty Deed (M.G.L. c. 183, § 10)

In Massachusetts, a warranty deed is analogous to a general warranty deed used in most states across the country. A warranty deed offers the buyer four warranty covenants when the deed is delivered. These are;

1. The grantor is the owner of the property in fee simple

2. The property concerned is free of any encumbrances besides those particularly described in the deed

3. The grantor holds the right for conveying the property to the grantee, his or her heirs and assigns

4. It is the duty of the grantor and his or her heirs to warrant and defend the title by countering any legal claims or demands from any other person arising before and until the grantor's lawful ownership of the property.

Quitclaim Deed (M.G.L. c. 183, § 11)

In Massachusetts, a quitclaim deed, unlike its equivalent used elsewhere across the country, is comparable to the special warranty deed commonly in use in most other states. The quitclaim deed used in Massachusetts offers the buyer two quitclaim or limited covenants when the deed is delivered. These are;

1. The grantor has not created any encumbrances over the land apart from those particularly expressed in the deed. Contrary to a special warranty deed used in most states, the quitclaim encompasses only encumbrances created by the grantor. It excludes other pre-existing encumbrances like easements, municipal limitations or restrictions, rights of way and such others.

2. The quitclaim deed provides the grantee the same force and effect as that of a deed in fee simple. It the grantor and his or her heirs' obligation to warrant and defend the grantee by countering any claims and demands, only for the period that the property is under the grantor's ownership.

Release Deed

In Massachusetts, a release deed is very much like the quitclaim deed used in many other states. A release deed facilitates the transfer of the grantor's right, title and interest, if any. No covenants or guarantees exist regarding the grantor possessing good title or any title, at all.

MASSACHUSETTS DEED VALIDATION REQUIREMENTS

A new deed is made and handed out every time the title is transferred. Any existing estate of homestead gets terminated automatically, if the owner and his or her spouse, if any, convey the real property through a deed.

➢ A deed has to be created in writing and must include the necessary language expressing grant or conveyance of the real property

➢ The grantor must adhere to the same name used at the time of taking the title. If the grantor's name while taking the title originally was different, then both the current name and original name of the grantor are required to be included in the deed. For example, if any woman acquires property prior to marriage and then marries, her pre-marriage and post-marriage names, both, must be incorporated in the conveyance deed

➢ The grantor is required to be lawfully competent

➢ The grantee should be alive and distinctly identifiable. The grantee's full name and address must be contained in the deed. If there are two or more grantees, then the deed must classify the co-ownership type.

➢ The deed must distinctly indicate the grantor's intention to convey the title. Under Massachusetts law, inserting the word "grant" is adequate and use of this word does not imply any covenant

➢ The deed must state the total value of the purchase transaction

➢ Every deed of unregistered land submitted for recording must necessarily contain the description of the property to be conveyed, in order to accurately and sufficient identify it. According to M.G.L. c. 183. § 6A, such descriptions must comprise references to previously recorded instruments or plans or those recorded along with the conveyance. M.G.L. c. 183, § 6 stipulates that the deed must state the street address of the concerned property, within the margin

➢ The conveyance deed is considered to be effective when it is handed over to and accepted by the grantee or his or her agent

➢ A deed for registered land has to be acknowledged in order to be recorded. Only after the deed gets recorded, the old certificate of title will be replaced with a new one proving the conveyance. In case of unregistered land, notarizing a deed to evidence the conveyance is optional, but it becomes mandatory if the deed has to be recorded. Under

Massachusetts law, notarizing a deed is not needed in order for it to be held valid. However, notarizing is mandatory in case it has to be recorded.

Note:

The title does not get transferred if a deed is recorded. The purpose of recording is simply to give intimation to the public or the world. The title is generally conveyed when the deed is delivered along with intent and acceptance.

WILL OR INHERITANCE

Under Massachusetts law, if a person dies leaving behind a Will, then such a person is termed to have died **testate**. A creator of a Will (testator) is required to be of minimum 18 years of age for the purpose of executing a written Will. The testator's signature must be witnessed by two or more lawfully competent individuals. At least two of the witnesses must not be benefitting in any manner from any *devise* or **legacy** arising out of the Will. Such two witnesses are required for the purposes of observing and confirming that the testator is giving his or her signature willfully and not under any duress and for witnessing their respective signatures. None of the witnesses has any rights of access to the contents of the Will. A surviving spouse possesses the right to challenge the contents of the Will and could get the provisions of the Will deemed invalid. In such cases, the surviving spouse could successfully resort to dower rights claim or gain up to 50 percent share of the property under specific conditions.

If a person dies without leaving a Will (**intestate**), then his or her property is dispersed in accordance with the state's intestate succession laws. The Massachusetts state law of Descent and Distribution concerning Real and Personal Property (M.G.L. c. 190) becomes applicable and generates a Will. In cases where a person dies intestate, the probate court designates an individual or entity to receive all claims pertaining to the estate. After repaying the dead person's debts, last illness and funeral charges and settlement of the land, any residual assets are dispersed as per the laws of the Commonwealth applicable under specific conditions, as below;

- ➢ Surviving spouse and progenies (children)

  The surviving spouse gets 50 percent of all real and personal property and the balance 50 percent is distributed equally among the children. Each child gets an equal share. In case, a child has died before the intestate then that child's offspring will receive his or her share. Both, biological as well as adopted children are treated as equals.

- ➢ Surviving spouse, no offspring or other relatives

  The surviving spouse gets ownership of all the real and personal property.

➢ Surviving spouse and relatives, but no offspring

If the intestate is survived by a spouse and some next of kin but not children, then the surviving spouse is eligible to receive the first $ 200,000 and 50 percent of the residual real and personal property. If the personal property is inadequate and falls short of $ 200,000, then the intestate's real property could be sold or mortgaged to raise that amount to be given to the surviving spouse. The residual 50 percent will be distributed to other family members (next of kin) in legal order as preferred.

➢ Surviving offspring, but predeceased spouse

All the real and personal property is distributed among the children. Each child is entitled to an equal share. In case, a child has died before the intestate, that child's offspring will receive his or her share. Both, biological as well as adopted children are considered equal.

➢ Surviving relatives, but predeceased spouse and no children

If a person dies intestate and has surviving relatives but no surviving spouse or offspring, then the real and personal property is bequeathed to the surviving relatives (next of kin) with the parents getting first right to it. If parents are predeceased, then the property is bestowed on the siblings and in case no siblings exist then the property is given to other family members in legal order of preference.

➢ Predeceased spouse and no surviving offspring or relatives

If an intestate does not have any surviving spouse or children or family members, then all real and personal property escheats to the Commonwealth

ADVERSE POSSESSION

Acquiring a property by physically dwelling in it for a continuous, prolonged period of time is known as *adverse possession*. Many of the states have laws that allow such acquisition of property. Adverse possession require the property to be occupied for a minimum of five years or more and this time period varies significantly across different states. Many states specify some other subsidiary necessities such as payment of real estate taxes. Under Massachusetts law, for obtaining a title to a property through adverse possession, the claimant is required to have physically resided in the property in an actual, open continuous, adverse-to-the-owner, notorious and exclusive manner for 20 years. Massachusetts law does not stipulate any subsidiary requirements, as do many other states. The claimant asserting adverse possession is under obligation to prove his or her claim. Property inhabited adversely can never be insured and no marketable title can be assigned to it until a legal title is acquired. The statutory requirement for claiming adverse possession of a property is its continuous occupancy for a period of 20 years. Continuity can be proven by tacking consecutive instances of adverse possession.

For example, Sarah adversely possesses a piece of land for a continuous period of 15 years and then passes it on to John, who, in turn, adversely possesses it for a further, continuous period of 5 years. In this case, John can claim the title to the piece of land through adverse possession by tacking the two successive occupancies.

The claimant is required to have exclusive possession and should have literally entered the property. If the entry into the property is simple infrequent or random, then it may be interpreted as trespass and the claim for adverse possession will not be held valid. But, seasonal or intermittent use of such property may be accepted for the purpose of establishing continuity, if the average owner uses a specific piece of property in that manner (e.g. as a summer lodging).

Possession has to be necessarily open and notorious. This means that the possession has to be noticeable and obvious. Possession only during the darkness of night is not considered as open and notorious.

Massachusetts laws do not recognize and permit adverse possession claims over some specific types of real property interests. These are;

> State highways (M.G.L. c. 81, § 22)

> Land under the ownership of railroads (M.G.L. c. 160, § 88)

> Registered land (M.G.L. c. 185, § 53)

> Conservation land under the ownership of non-profit corporations (M.G.L. c. 260, § 21)

> Public burial grounds (refer case: 84 Mass. (2 Allen) 512 (1861), Commonwealth v. Viall)

> Land under the ownership of United States (refer case: 886 F.2d 448 (1st Cir. 1989), United States v. Hato Rey Bldg. Co.)

> Land under the ownership of the Commonwealth and being used for the purpose of conservation or other public benefit (M.G.L. c. 260, § 31)

EMINENT DOMAIN

The government is empowered to take private property for public use. This power is known as *eminent domain*. The power to take public property for public purposes arises from the US constitution, state constitutions, federal and state laws (M.G.L. c. 79). Local governments such as cities, towns and counties as well, possess the power of eminent domain.

For example, if the Massachusetts Highway Department requires a portion of a property for a public use, it is empowered to take the title of that property from its lawful owner by eminent domain.

The process of eminent domain involves the following steps;

1. The taking authority will first hire the services of a real estate appraiser to assess the property's fair market value. If this task involves complexities, it may hire the services of engineers and other experts to aid the appraiser to arrive at the property's fair market value.

2. Next, it will draw out a taking plan, which will precisely indicate the property to be taken.

3. Then, a title search is performed on the property to identify the property's owners and other individuals or entities, which may hold an interest in the property.

4. The taking order is then recorded at the registry deeds linked to the location of the property. The recording of the taking order serves as a deed, conveying such property's title from its owner to the taking authority.

5. A notice of taking is now sent to the property owner informing that his or her property is taken.

6. Finally, the property owner, whose property is taken, is offered payment as per the fair market value determined by the taking authority.

Fair Market Value or "just compensation"

According to Massachusetts courts, the "just compensation" of fair market value is defined as the "the highest price that a hypothetical willing buyer will pay or offer to a hypothetical willing seller in an assumed free and open market" (Epstein v. Boston Housing Authority, 317 Mass. 297 (1944)). This means that the value of the property has to be assessed on the exact date that it was taken, as if the property was sold in the free and open market. Further, the price should have been arrived at by fully informed and willing parties, not under any kind of duress to buy or sell, on the valuation date. The objective is to determine the highest price for the property taken that a buyer would agree to pay and the seller would agree to accept.

Valuation Date or "taking date"

The fair market value of the property taken, which is due to the property owner, is determined on the date on which the taking order is recorded. This date is known as the valuation date or "taking date". Thus the fair market value of the property is arrived at by assuming that a hypothetical sale occurred on the date of recording the taking order in the registry of deeds.

"pro tanto" Payment

When the taking authority offers a fair market value, determined by it, to the property owner for the property taken, the property owner reserves the right to accept the amount offered as either full compensation or as "pro tanto". This means that it is accepted as partial payment as in the owner's opinion, the amount offered is insufficient and misrepresents the fair market value for the property taken. In Latin, the phrase "pro tanto" means "so far" or "to that extent" and denotes that the payment offered by the taking authority is accepted by the property owner as only a portion of the "just compensation" that he or she is entitled to. By accepting a payment "pro tanto", the property owner reserves the right to file a lawsuit against the taking authority in less than three (3) years from the recording date of the taking order in the registry of deeds and such a lawsuit is decided by a judge or jury.

The taking authority is required to pay for the property within sixty (60) days from the recording date of the taking order in the registry of deeds. In case of delay beyond 60 days, the taking authority has to pay interest on the pro tanto amount for the period between the taking date and the actual date of payment.

Halting Eminent Domain

The United States and Massachusetts laws hold valid exercising of the power of eminent domain, if it is for public purpose. The taking authority usually fulfills such public purpose requirements when it takes property to protect or promote public safety, health and welfare. For example, widening of roads, protecting the environment or redeveloping decadent areas are typical public purpose projects. Recently, the U.S. Supreme Court decisions have vastly extended the scope of valid public purpose projects, making it extremely difficult to halt eminent domain takings.

Under Massachusetts law, if a person dies intestate and has no known legal heirs then the property of the deceased transfers (escheats) to the state. In several other states, such property generally transfers to the county. Thereafter, the Commonwealth has complete power to either retain or dispose it off. This concept of escheat has its roots in the English law which believes that truly orphaned real property could be harmful to public interests.

FORECLOSURE

When the terms of a mortgage or promissory note are dishonored and a default occurs, the mortgagee may opt for an **entry and possession** or **non-judicial foreclosure** within **power-of-sale clause** or both.

Generally, standard mortgages and notes have a provision of issuing an initial default notice to the mortgagor. The notice generally states a specific time period within which the mortgagor is required to set right the default and prevent foreclosure. Such a notice is usually issued before the foreclosure is referred to an attorney. Until the end of the time period stated in the notice, the foreclosure process cannot be started.

Entry and Possession

Entry and possession is rarely used as the initial method of foreclosure. However, it serves as a backup in case of a procedural mistake during the non-judicial sale process. The entry can only be achieved after a time period of three years. This means that any time during these three years, the mortgagor is allowed to redeem the property by repaying all the dues to the mortgagee. The entry must necessarily be witnessed by two persons. There are three ways to affect entry and possession:

1. File a lawsuit to obtain a court order giving the lender possession.

2. Enter peaceably and take possession

3. Obtain borrowers consent to entry

Non-Judicial Foreclosure

In case of non-judicial foreclosure, the mortgagee can resort to the acceleration clause, which requires the entire debt, as per the promissory note, to become due and payable immediately. The power-of-sale clause included in the mortgage authorizes beforehand the sale of the property in order to recover the outstanding portion of the mortgage loan in case the mortgagor defaults. The foreclosure sale has to be conducted in the exact manner as stated in the power-of-sale clause. The mortgagee is required to strictly adhere to the process, as stated below.

1. Try to obtain a judgment to foreclose the mortgage by filing a petition in the land court (both, superior court as well as the Massachusetts Supreme Judicial Court hold jurisdiction, but seldom used). The purpose of this process is to ensure that the owner (s) of the property do not possess any right to seek relief according to the Service Members Civil Relief Act (SCRA). The court will then issue an Order of Notice as per this process.

2. Get the Order of Notice recorded in the county in which the property is located. The Order of Notice includes the names of the parties, the full address of the property, and the book as well as the page number on which the mortgage is recorded.

3. Issue a Notice of Sale through registered or certified mail, a minimum of 14 days before the sale date, to the mortgagor as well as all record owners and junior lien holders.

4. Print the Notice of Sale in a popular, local newspaper with significant circulation, once every week over three consecutive weeks. The first publication must appear in the newspaper at least 21 days before the sale date.

5. Issue a special notice of probable delinquency to the mortgagor, a minimum of 21 days before the scheduled sale date, in case the mortgagee wishes to retain the right to obtain a deficiency judgment. A separate lawsuit, within a period of two years from the sale date, is necessary to be filed by the mortgagee in order to pursue a deficiency judgment.

6. Effect the sale through a public auction on the date and time specified in the Notice of Sale. The sale has to be conducted at or in close proximity to the site of the property, which forms the subject of the foreclosure.

7. Have the sale conducted by a licensed auctioneer and ensure that the property is sold to the highest bidder.

8. Register a copy of the Notice of Sale along with an affidavit declaring that the foreclosure process was conducted lawfully, within 30 days from the sale date.

Note:

1. With reference to step 1 above; The Service Members Civil Relief Act (SCRA) was signed into law H.R. 100 by the president of the United States on December 19, 2003. This law completely restructured the Soldiers and Sailors Civil Relief Act of 1940 by extending the scope of several civil protections included in the previous law. In January

2013, Thomas Kennedy put forth Billl S.753 (An Act to amend the foreclosure statute to require judicial foreclosure)

SENATE DOCKET, NO. 443   FILED ON: 1/16/2013

SENATE . . . . No. 753

The Commonwealth of Massachusetts

PRESENTED BY:

Thomas P. Kennedy

To the Honorable Senate and House of Representatives of the Commonwealth of Massachusetts in General Court assembled:

The undersigned legislators and/or citizens respectfully petition for the adoption of the accompanying bill:

An Act to amend the foreclosure statute to require judicial foreclosure.

PETITION OF:

NAME:	DISTRICT/ADDRESS:
Thomas P. Kennedy	*Second Plymouth and Bristol*
Kay Khan	*11th Middlesex*
Gale D. Candaras	*First Hampden and Hampshire*

SENATE DOCKET, NO. 443   FILED ON: 1/16/2013

SENATE . . . . No. 753

By Mr. Kennedy, a petition (accompanied by bill, Senate, No. 753) of Thomas P. Kennedy, Kay Khan and Gale D. Candaras for legislation to amend the foreclosure statute to require judicial foreclosure. The Judiciary.

[SIMILAR MATTER FILED IN PREVIOUS SESSION
SEE SENATE, NO. *809* OF 2011-2012.]

The Commonwealth of Massachusetts

In the Year Two Thousand Thirteen

An Act to amend the foreclosure statute to require judicial foreclosure.

Be it enacted by the Senate and House of Representatives in General Court assembled, and by the authority of the same, as follows:

SECTION 1. Chapter 244 is hereby amended by inserting after Section 1 the following section:–

Section 2: Foreclosure by Complaint: All foreclosures of residential mortgages on 1-4 family owner-occupied properties shall be initiated by the filing of a foreclosure complaint against the mortgagor in the superior court for the county in which the property is located. Such filing shall include notice pursuant to 50 U.S.C. App. sec. 501 et seq., the Service Members Civil Relief Act ("SCRA") as it exists or may be amended, and no additional filing in the Land Court, pursuant to SCRA shall be required. A defendant-residential mortgagor may raise all legal and equitable claims and defenses. The court shall have the authority to modify the mortgage or grant any other appropriate relief as to the mortgagor but nothing in this section shall affect the rights of tenants or other legal occupants residing in the property that is the subject of the complaint. The court may set aside a default judgment for good cause shown.

Bill History

Bill S.753   188th (Current)

An Act to amend the foreclosure statute to require judicial foreclosure

By Mr. Kennedy, a petition (accompanied by bill, Senate, No. 753) of Thomas P. Kennedy, Kay Khan and Gale D. Candaras for legislation to amend the foreclosure statute to require judicial foreclosure. The Judiciary.

Sponsors: Thomas P. Kennedy

Status: Referred to Joint Committee on the Judiciary

Current Bill Text	**Bill History**	Miscellaneous	🖨 Print Preview

Actions for Bill S.753

Date	Branch	Action
1/22/2013	Senate	Referred to the committee on The Judiciary
1/22/2013	House	House concurred
6/11/2013	Joint	Hearing scheduled for 06/19/2013 from 01:00 PM-05:00 PM in A-1
3/20/2014	House	Reporting date extended to Monday June 30, 2014, pending concurrence
4/3/2014	Senate	Senate concurred

The information contained in this website is for general information purposes only. The General Court provides this information as a public service and while we endeavor to keep the data accurate and current to the best of our ability, we make no representations or warranties of any kind, express or implied, about the completeness, accuracy, reliability, suitability or availability with respect to the website or the information contained on the website for any purpose. Any reliance you place on such information is therefore strictly at your own risk.

2. With reference to step 2 above; The purpose of the Notice of Sale is to ensure that the mortgagee makes a diligent and conscious attempt to locate and establish contact with the borrower. However, it is not necessary that the borrower should actually receive the notice in order to conduct the sale.

Excess Sale Proceeds

If the proceeds realized from the foreclosure sale are in excess, after accounting for the outstanding debt and costs, then such excess proceeds are first dispersed among the junior lien holders, if any, as per priority. Thereafter, any residual proceeds or the complete surplus, in case no junior lien holders exist, is handed over to the former mortgagor.

Redemption Rights

Under Massachusetts law, the mortgagor does not enjoy and statutory rights of redemption post-sale. But the mortgagor retains a justifiable right of redemption until the sale, to recover all the defaults related to the loan.

Deficient Sale Proceeds

If the proceeds resulting from the foreclosure sale fall short of meeting the mortgage obligations, then the mortgagee has the option of filing a suit against the mortgagor to obtain a deficiency judgment and recover the unpaid dues within a period of two years from the date of the foreclosure sale.

Default Notice (M.G.L. c. 244, § 35A)

Effective May 1, 2008, a new law has come into existence requiring a new notice of default that is applicable to owner-occupied residential property comprising one-to-four-dwelling units. A mortgagee is required to give a 90-day notice providing an opportunity to mend a payments default through full repayment of amounts due without inflation of the pending balance of the mortgage loan. The 90-day right to mend a default can be exercised only once within a five-year period. The law has provision to offer the mortgagor a list of particular disclosure information. Between this 90-day period and before inflation,

> ➤ The mortgagor need not pay any charges, fees or penalty linked to exercising the right to mend a default

> ➤ The mortgagor can pay late fees and interest charges per diem to mend the default

> ➤ The mortgagor does not incur any liability to pay attorneys' fees concerning the default during the 90-day time frame

> ➤ The mortgagee may choose to reinstate the mortgage loan after the end of the 90-day notice period

> ➤ A copy of the 90-day notice must be filed by the mortgagee with the commissioner of the division of banks

Foreclosed Property Tenancy (M.G.L. c. 186, §§ 13, 13A)

When a foreclosure sale results in sale of a property, the leases of some tenants residing on the property could get terminated and their tenancies may be converted to month-to-month or tenant-at-will. The leases impacted are usually those with a fixed unexpired term. A foreclosure does not affect any lease agreements if the rental payments are subsidized in accordance with state and federal law. Consequently, after a foreclosure all other leases are converted to or retained as month-to-month tenancies. All the terms and conditions of such tenancies are carried forward indefinitely unless either party issues a proper notice to the other. The notice becomes effective on the due date of the next rental after an advance notice period of 30 days. The minimum notice period is 30 days. But in the case of rooming houses, where the rent is collected on a weekly or daily basis, the notice period is *seven* days. A tenant can be removed or evicted under any and all circumstances only through a valid court order.

Tenant at Sufferance

A former mortgagor, whose property has been lawfully sold through a foreclosure sale, can be evicted from the premises only through a summary process and a proper court order.

Notice of Accounts (M.G.L. c. 183, § 27)building code

The mortgagee is required to give the mortgagor a written notice that includes an itemized account of the dispersal of the proceeds realized from a foreclosure sale. Such a notice must necessarily contain the sale price; publication costs; legal, auctioneer and other fees; and any balance to be handed over to the mortgagor. This notice must be issued within a period of 60 days after such funds are received.

Note:

M.G.L. c. 244, § 14A stipulates that the Commissioner of the Division of Banks is required to maintain a foreclosure database which lists all the foreclosure transactions done by mortgage holders, lenders, servicers, brokers and loan originators, who deposited their mortgage loans in the Common wealth. The commissioner must generate a report, at least once a year, for observing the trends and developments in mortgage foreclosures related to residential property within the Commonwealth and such a report must be made available to the general public upon request.

ENCUMBRANCES AND LIENS

On reading this section completely, you will understand;

- What is an Easement
- Different types of Easements
- What is a License

ENCUMBRANCES

Encumbrances are an interest in a particular land that places a burden on the current value. There are four primary types of encumbrances:

1) Legal attachments, mortgages, tax liens, and mechanics liens

2) Easements

3) Encroachments

4) Deed restrictions

Legal attachments. An attachment is a legal process by which a defendant real estate is used as security for the satisfaction of a dick or judgment. The attachment is initiated to prevent the defendant from hiding assets or transferring title to another. Constructive notice of the attachment is made by recording a lis pendens (suit pending) at the Registry of Deeds. An attachment is involuntary lien. An attachment may be general or special.

Mortgage. A mortgage is a voluntary contract that creates a special lien. A mortgage is a lien to secure the repayment a loan.

Liens arise from debt that are owed. Liens can be created by agreement (voluntary) or by operation of law (Involuntary).

Municipal liens. Municipal liens are used to secure the payment of real estate taxes, water and sewer charges, and special assessments for public projects.

Government liens. Government lands are filed by federal and state government for the non-payment of income taxes and some employer payroll taxes.

Mechanics liens (M.G.L.c. 254). In mechanics lien is a special lien created to ensure payment for materials supply in the improvement, or repair of real property. There must be an express or implied contract between the contractor/supplier in the property owner. Note: subcontractors also have a lien against the owner and do not have to go through the primary contractor in order to effect payment. A mechanics lien must be filed within a specific Time after performance has commenced or ended, And a notice of any claim must be filed with the Registry of Deeds. In Massachusetts a civil action may be found in Superior Court in order to have the mechanics lien enforced. Liens on Buildings and Land http://www.lawlib.state.ma.us/subject/about/mechanics.html

Note: buyers of recently constructed or repaired properties should obtain an affidavit from the seller to ensure that no work has been performed on the property within the last 45 days of the closing.

Judgments. A judgment is a verdict that money is old by the debtor to a creditor. Payment of any unpaid judgment is recoverable through court action in Massachusetts. A writ of execution must be obtained to direct the Sheriff to seize and sell the debtors property in order to satisfy the debt. Note: in Massachusetts a debtor has one year following a Sheriff's sale to pay the debt plus interest and costs in order to redeem the title.

Discharge of Liens

Liens may be discharged by way of the following:

1. Payment/satisfaction of the debt incurred.

2. By agreement of the parties.

3. Dissolution by operation of law (such as through civil or Superior Court).

4. By filing an acceptable bond.

EASEMENT

An easement is a property right that is non-possessory and grants its holder, an interest in land belonging to another person. Such land encumbered by an easement is known as "servient estate" (tenement) and the person or land, which benefits from the easement, is called "dominant estate" (tenement). The easement that benefits a specific piece of adjoining land is deemed to be appurtenant to that land and if the easement benefits only a particular person or business then it is called *"in gross"*.

Majority of easements are affirmative, that is, they permit usage of land owned by another person or entity. *Negative easements* involve protecting a person's access to light or a particular view by restricting the rights of usage (such as constructing a building) on abutting or neighboring land. Such easements are less common.

According to Massachusetts law, a property simply having windows overlooking an adjacent land does not acquire an intrinsic easement of light or air which can restrict the erection of a building (M.G.L.c. 187, § 1).

Easements can be created in only the following three ways, under Massachusetts law;

1. By deed or express grant

2. By prescription (adverse usage)

3. By necessity (implicit easement)

Easement in Gross

An easement in gross is a personal right with limitations, granted to benefit a person or business. The direct benefits accrue to the holder of the easement instead of another parcel of land. An easement in gross is distinctly different from an appurtenant easement in terms of a lack of dominant estate in the former. Easements in gross are often used for sewer, storm drains, public water, electricity, television, cable, phone and such other utility service. Such easements are usually documented in the public records for every property title that is impacted. Under Massachusetts law, an easement in gross rendered invalid automatically if is remains unused for the planned purpose for a period of 30 years (M.G.L. c. 184A, § 5)

Exclusions: Some examples of instances that are not recognized as uses by utilities are; the permission to erect an advertising billboard (outdoor sign) and the right to swim in a water body owned by another person or entity.

Negative Easements

Easements are usually affirmative, permitting the enjoyment of another's land through easement in gross, appurtenant easement, easement by necessity and prescriptive easement. Besides these, there exist negative or restrictive easements under Massachusetts law. The negative easement holder enjoys the right to restrict any activity on the servient estate by the possessor of the servient tenement. Negative easements may be viewed by some courts as restrictions that are not enforceable.

See: Myers v. Salin, 13 Mass.App.Ct. 127, 431 N.E.2d. 233 (1992) *by Deed, Prescription, Necessity*

EASEMENT BY DEED *(M.G.L.c. 187, § 2)*

A vast majority of the easements are created by deed or through express grant. The grantors may transfer a limited easement right on their property. Alternatively, the grantors may transfer all their rights related to a particular property except retaining an easement. The assignees, heirs and grantees could benefit from an easement indefinitely. An easement may be granted for a specific or limited duration. An easement refers to an interest in land and the Statute of Frauds stipulates that it must be in writing in order to be enforceable.

EASEMENT BY PRESCRIPTION *(M.G.L.c. 187, § 2)*

A prescriptive easement is obtained through adverse usage (without permission from the owner) of the land belonging to another person. Under Massachusetts law, such adverse use is required to be uninterrupted for 20 years. Almost all states grant prescriptive easements, however, the required usage tenure differs across states.

Requirements: Massachusetts law requires a claim for prescriptive easement to be hostile, notorious, open, actual, continuous and uninterrupted for 20 years.

Registered Land: A prescriptive easement is not applicable to registered land.

Tacking: This refers to the sum of periods of prescriptive use by continuous users when the interest in property of such continuous users has overtaken the interest of previous owners or users through modes such as a deed, will or inheritance. Tacking is permitted for proving the mandatory 20 years of continuous use.

Privity is essential for tacking. Privity of title or possession indicates mutual or successive interests in the same piece of land or real property.

EASEMENT BY NECESSITY

According to Massachusetts law, if a piece of land is landlocked then an easement may be inferred. Usually, whenever a transfer results in a landlocked parcel of land with no way of access whatsoever other than through the servient tenement retained by the seller or through the land of another person (stranger), the necessity may be acknowledged.

➢ Easement by necessity cannot be inferred and hence cannot be acquired for registered land.

➢ Easement by necessity is never granted automatically, but must come into effect through a court order. Each case is reviewed according to its circumstances. Factors such as parties' intent, land layout, buyer and seller knowledge and actual conveyance document references together have a vital bearing on the judicial decision.

➢ Easements by necessity are frequently inferred to allow access to a landlocked property. Easement by necessity is akin to an easement by implication, however, it is considered only when deemed strictly necessary. An easement by implication may be created when the use of the dominant tenement becomes necessary for complete usage of the land, such as carrying utility items to the dominant tenement.

LICENSE

This is the smallest right under Massachusetts laws of real estate. It confers the right to occupy land. It is neither an easement nor a lease. It does not indicate an interest in real estate but simply means a personal and general (non-exclusive) contract. Massachusetts law allows termination of a license to occupy real property, by either party and at any time, irrespective of any oral or written agreement between them.

DOWER AND CURTESY RIGHTS

On reading this section completely, you will understand;

- What are dower and curtesy rights
- What is tenancy as per dower rights
- The current status of dower and curtesy rights, especially in Massachusetts

Dower (wife) and Curtesy (husband) are longstanding common-law models concerning the separation of marital property. The principles were used for protecting both spouses involved in a marriage from the possible scenario where the other disinherits the property. Curtesy denotes the husband's rights in his wife's property and dower denotes the wife's rights in her husband's property. Dower and curtesy, both, have now become obsolete, in modern times. In fact, most of the states have abolished both these laws completely. Laws pertaining to descent and distribution, use of joint tenancies, divorce and property settlements, tenancies by the entirety and tenancies-in-common have ensured prevention of situations where the surviving spouse is left without a part in the marital property.

Tenancy by Dower (M.G.L.c. 189, § 1)

Massachusetts abolished majority of the dower and curtesy rights in 1966 with the exception of such lands that were under ownership at the time of death. In addition, the government has removed the differentiation between dower and curtesy. Any residual rights are now only referred to as **dower**, a gender-neutral name. In modern times, the term **dower** is seldom used and is commonly called *spouse's statutory share*. In a deed, attaining a discharge of dower or curtesy rights is no longer required because dower rights begin only on death. The spouse's statutory share (dower rights) in existence in Massachusetts today, offer life estate to a surviving spouse, which consists of one third of the total land owned by the late spouse until death.

> ➤ A surviving spouse is not allowed to claim division of assets as specified in the Massachusetts Law of Descent and Distribution (M.G.L.c. 190) in case he or she chooses to accept the benefits of dower rights.

> ➤ Under Massachusetts law, divorce terminates dower rights (M.G.L.c. 208, §27).

Massachusetts is not amongst the list of nine states that consider community property for the purpose of defining marital property.

Current community property states include:

Arizona
California
Idaho
Louisiana
Nevada
New Mexico
Texas
Washington
Wisconsin

WATER RIGHTS

On reading this section completely, you will understand;

- What are Riparian rights and where do they apply
- What are Littoral rights and where do they apply
- The clear differences between Riparian and Littoral rights and their significance under Massachusetts laws

Massachusetts as well as Maine (formerly included under Massachusetts) have been distinctly different from other states, anywhere in the country, in terms of offering highly restrictive public access to beaches. All other states permit private ownership to extend only up to the mean high-water mark. Massachusetts and Maine exclusively permit private ownership up to the mean low-water mark. This essentially prohibits public access and mobility along private beaches.

RIPARIAN

Massachusetts is known as a riparian state. Frequently, the term riparian rights means and includes all rights pertaining to water-front. However, there is distinct difference between riparian and littoral rights (explained below).

Riparian rights are the rights and obligations of a property owner, in land that borders or surrounds a river, stream or such other water body. These rights permit access to as well as use of the water.

A riparian owner holds the right to use and relish the stream, but is not allowed to divert its flow. In case of navigable streams the riparian rights owner usually owns the land leading up to the water's edge and the ownership of the land under the water lies with the public. In case of non-navigable streams, the riparian rights owner owns the land up to the middle of the stream. Alternatively, if the riparian rights owner is the owner of land on both the sides of the stream then the riparian owner is the owner of all the land under the water as well.

Wetlands are strictly regulated by the Massachusetts Department of Environmental Protection. Any attempt to reclaim wetlands by filling up without mandatory permits is illegal.

The state regulates all surface waters such as ponds and lakes. The land up to the water's edge is owned by the riparian owner.

LITTORAL

Littoral rights are the rights and obligations of a property owner, in land that borders a sea, ocean, large lake or such other still or tidal waters.

Tidal Water (M.G.L.c. 91, §1)

Tideland, is the legal term which means present and former submerged lands and tidal flats below the mean high water mark (between the high-tide and low-tide marks).

Private Tideland, in Massachusetts, refers to the intertidal zone between the high and low water marks defined within M.G.L. c. 91, §1 as "tidelands held by a private party subject to an easement of the public for the purposes of navigation and free fishing and fowling and of passing freely over and through the water."

The littoral rights owner owns the land leading up to the mean low-water mark, but not more than 1650 feet (100 rods) beyond the high-water mark, towards the sea.

Use of Private Tidelands

A long-standing Massachusetts law provides a public easement for navigation, fowling and free fishing along private beaches. This could be interpreted to mean that a person travelling in a boat or carrying a gun, binoculars or a fishing rod holds the right o exercise the right of easement but is not allowed to occupy the property. In the past, the courts and / or the attorney general have been lenient in their rulings regarding this right, as below;

- ✓ Swimming: Since the water is not under private ownership, beachgoers are allowed to swim anywhere. But if the swimmers touch the private tidelands then they are said to have committed a trespass theoretically.

- ✓ Fishing: The right to fish is inclusive of the right to seek or carry any fish or shellfish on foot or from a vessel (boat etc.).

- ✓ Navigate: The right to navigate is inclusive of the right to perform any activity that involves mobility of a boat, windsurfer, sail, float or any type of vessel.

- ✓ Fowling: The right to fowl encompasses the right to hunt birds as a sport and for sustenance. (The attorney general is of the opinion that the right of fowling covers bird watching).

However, the courts have consistently ruled that the public right towards usage of private tidelands does not cover the right to simply stroll, sunbathe or engage in any other recreational activity not related to fishing, fowling and navigation. Such general recreation, without the permission of the land owner, is considered as trespassing. But, the public always has the right to walk, swim or indulge in other recreational activities, below the low-water line (or 100 rods (1650 feet) towards the sea, after the high-water mark). Such tidelands, towards the land and up to the low-water line, belong to the state, with a few exceptions.

CHAPTER 2

KEY TERMS

condominium	options	gross
cooperative	assign	Triple net
Time share	sublet	Security deposit
Leases	Ninety-nine year lease	Obligation of the parties
tenancy	Lead paint	Right of first refusal

CHAPTER 2 LEARNING OBJECTIVES

Upon your completion of this chapter you should be able to:

1. Comprehend laws to form condominiums
2. Distinguish between Unit Deed and Master Deed
3. What is a stock certificate in corporation?
4. What is a proprietary unit lease?
5. The definition of weekly ownership of timeshares.
6. The role of exchange organizations.
7. What are freehold and non-freehold properties?
8. The meaning of Lessor, Lessee, Term, Lease and Demised.
9. What is tenancy for years?
10. What is tenancy from period to period?
11. What is the meaning of tenancy at Will?
12. What does tenancy at sufferance mean?
13. The habitability requirements and the State Sanitary Code.
14. What is the Right of First Refusal?
15. The key responsibilities of property management.
16. Identify key differences in common leases.
17. What is a 99 year lease?
18. Laws related to Smoke Detectors.
19. Laws pertaining to Discrimination

CONDOMINIUMS/COOPERATIVES/TIME SHARING/ LAND USE – SUBDIVISION

CONDOMINIUMS

Condominiums (M.G.L. c. 183A)

Condo owners purchase their units in the same manner as a detached residence. Unit owners pay a monthly fee for the maintenance of common areas. Condo fees vary by association and may include costs for master insurance, snow and trash removal, repairs, parking and common area maintenance.

On reading this section completely, you will understand;

- How condominium Master Deed, By-laws and other Rules and Regulations are formulated?
- The difference between Unit Deed and Master Deed.
- The process of preparing condominium budget.
- What is percentage of common ownership?
- What constitutes common areas in a condominium?
- The role of trustees in managing Condo Associations.
- Implications of mortgage and maintenance fee default.
- What are closing documents – 6d and Insurance certificates?

CREATION--MASTER DEED, BY-LAW, RULES AND REGULATIONS

A new condo development requires: creation and public recording of a master deed, formation of an association, rules and regulations (bylaws) and unit deeds.

Creation – Master Deed

The rights of unit owners is defined by the master deed.

A condominium is created when the set of condominium documents, which include the master deed, the overall site plan and the master plan of each floor, are submitted and recorded at the registry of deeds. The master deed clearly draws out and determines the common areas, the boundaries, location and number of each individual condominium unit and specifies the rights and obligations applicable to all unit owners.

A statement of purpose is generally included to inform owners of restrictions of use for each unit, if any.

The Master Deed is also used to convert and existing building to a condominium.

By-Laws

The by-laws determine the rules, regulations and processes for the governance and functioning of the owners' association. The condominium owners' association is formed through the Declaration of Trust. This declaration of trust, including the by-laws, is recorded along with the master deed.

Bylaws generally include the following:

1. Restrictions and requirements for the use and maintenance of units and common areas.

2. Method and manner of collecting unit owner fees and expenses.

3. Procedure for hiring personnel.

4. Procedure for adopting and amending rules that govern the use of common areas.

Rules & Regulation

The declaration of trust includes the components of common expenses that are to be paid such as the general maintenance charges, the water and sewer charges and the master insurance premium, all pertaining to the common areas. The by-laws specify the rules and regulation applicable for condominium governance and day-to-day functioning.

UNIT DEED VS MASTER DEED

- ✓ The Unit Deed pertains to an individual condominium unit; while the Master Deed pertains to the entire set of condominiums constructed.

- ✓ The Unit Deed includes the property description or the post-office address and the details of the Master Deed registry record such as book, page and date, while the Master Deed contains the drawings and specifications of individual condominium units including boundaries and common areas.

✓ The Unit Deed contains the references in the Master Deed for a particular condominium unit as well as other details that identify that particular unit; while the Master Deed contains details for the entire facility and each condominium unit.

✓ The Unit Deed includes the statement of intended use of particular condominium unit and applicable usage restrictions, if any; while the Master Deed includes the statement of purpose of the entire condominiums facility and owners' rights and obligations.

✓ The Unit Deed specifies the owner's interest in the facilities and common areas related to an individual unit; while the Master Deed defines owners' interests and duties with respect to facilities and common areas for all condominium units.

It is mandatory for the first unit deed of every individual condominium unit to include extracts from the master deed highlighting the portions of the plans that depict the particular unit being conveyed and the immediate adjoining units. It must completely and precisely display the unit's key parameters such as the layout, size, dimensions, location, main entrance and surrounding accessible common areas.

BUDGET PREPARATION

Condominium associations vary in size from very small consisting just 2 – 3 units to very large consisting of hundreds of units. For small associations written budgets rarely exist but for large associations budget preparation involves professionals. Fannie Mae, the apex firm passing mortgages, does not require a written budget for condominiums with 2 – 4 units but requires one from associations with 5 or more condominium units. Many lenders often require a written budget even for associations with 2 – 4 units. Hence it is a good practice to have a written budget irrespective of the size of the association.

In today's scenario, it is the prospective buyer and the buyer's lender who usually express interest in reviewing the budget. What they are looking for mainly is the line item indicating 10% reserve. The regular recurring expenses are met by 90% of the fees collected annually and 10% is required to be saved as a reserve in a separate reserve account. Although many lenders do not insist on a separate reserve account, buyers planning to obtain mortgage guarantees from the FHA (Federal Housing Administration) require condominium associations to adhere to specified norms strictly.

The key elements of the budget are;

➢ Reserves.

➢ Capital – funds allotted for maintaining the common areas.

> ➤ Contingency Reserves – covers emergencies that are unforeseen and not provisioned for in the budget.

> ➤ Condominium Fees – determined on the basis of the calculations of the annual budget and collected monthly from each unit owner. The share of each owner is directly proportional to the percentage interest of the owner.

All regular recurring expenses such as water and sewer, insurance, common electricity bill and definitely recurring expenses such as snow removal have to be budgeted for and included in a line item. Some accountants include a line item titled 'maintenance' to provision funds for general maintenance purposes. Expenses not incurred every year may not be budgeted for in advance and the same can be met from the reserves. For example, if the association plans to install play equipment for children worth $10000 in the approaching year, then the budget for that year can still indicate a 10% reserve. The following year's budget can indicate that the money was spent out of reserves.

The annual budget is a yearly feature and is the blueprint for the condominium community. It determines the financial health, or lack of it, for the condominium associations in the approaching as well as subsequent years. Every annual budget is unique similar to its community and a painless, efficient budgeting process can be set up in various ways. Some communities may attribute its budgeting success to its active board of directors while others may emphasize the importance of unit owners' feedback.

PERCENT OF COMMON OWNERSHIP

(M.G.L. c. 183A, §5)

Each individual condominium unit is nominated an undivided ownership of the common areas in accordance with the percentage specified in the master deed. This percentage determines the vote size entitlement of the unit owner in the condominium association business as well as the budget percentage (amount) that the unit owner is required to contribute (pay).

In Massachusetts, this percentage of common ownership is determined and recorded at the same date as that of the original master deed. This percentage value is calculated in the same proportion that fair value of the individual unit bears to the fair value of all the units taken together. The percentage of common ownership in the common areas for an individual unit, as specified in the master deed, can only be changed with the approval of all the unit owners and their respective mortgagees since it has a material impact on their undivided interest. Only a successful vote can lead to an appropriate amendment in the master deed.

Ownership is represented by deed. Units are generally held in fee simple, subject to restrictive covenants and conditions. Condo units are sometimes referred to as horizontal ownership (due to resemblance to cubicle like spaces).

CONDOMINIUM FEES

Condo fees are interchangeable with the following: association dues, maintenance charges, condominium dues. Each unit owner is required to pay a pro-rate share of the common expenses.

CONDOMINIUM REAL ESTATE TAXES

Each unit owner is responsible for the assessed taxes on individual units. The common area taxes are included in the association fees. Each unit is assigned a proportionate percentage.

COMMON AREAS

The common areas comprise the entire condominium project except the separate interests of individual unit owners. Common areas include building's exterior portions, lobbies, walkways, hallways, elevators, lawn, supporting walls, parking lot, swimming pools and other recreational facilities. All the owners are allowed to make use of the common areas and have to share the costs of operating and maintaining them. NOTE: Parking spaces may be both a common element or rented in addition to the living unit.

ASSOCIATION AND MANAGEMENT--TRUSTEES

Condominium associations are organizations set up for the purpose of owning and governing the common areas in the condominium. In Massachusetts, it is usually in the form of a 'trust'. In the case of larger condominiums, the unit owners appoint the trustees (board members) through a vote at an annual meeting. The Declaration of Trust (Corporate By-laws) establish the terms of office and conditions for resignation, removal or replacement of trustees. In the case of smaller associations, the condominium documents provision for the owners of individual units must appoint a trustee. In this case, the unit owner must appoint the trustee in writing and record it in the relevant registry of deeds. The unit owners have to meet annually to vote for the trustees (board members) and approve major amendments to the Declaration of Trust. The trustees are empowered by the Declaration of Trust to manage the day-to-day affairs of the condominium.

The trustees oversee the governance of the condominium association on behalf of the unit owners. There can be one or more condominium units. These details are included in the Master

Deed and the Declaration of Trust. Responsibilities of the trustees include conducting meetings, collecting monthly fees, handling the bank account, issuing 6D certificates, managing lawsuits and in general, enforcing rules and regulations applicable to condominiums. In larger condominiums, the trustees hire a property manager to manage the day-to-day affairs and tasks.

The trustees are personally liable for specific negligent and inappropriate acts. However, in Massachusetts, it is common practice to include in the condominium documents, provisions to shield the trustees from such liabilities. Some of the common provisions in the trusteeship documents pertaining to condominiums are;

➢ Right to Resign - Trustees should have the option to resign in case difficult or risky situations arise.

➢ Indemnification – This is the most important clause, which is included in almost all the Massachusetts condominium declarations. This clause protects the trustees if they commit a mistake. If a trustee commits and error, which is not embezzlement or some deliberate violation of rules and regulations, the condominium association will bear the costs incurred.

➢ Conflict of Interest – This clause safeguards the validity of the trustees' actions. With this clause included, any action that a trustee may take which would favor him / her individually as a unit owner cannot be reversed.

With the inclusion of the above clauses, the trustees enjoy the right to mitigated liability. As a general rule, the trustee does not have the right to receive any payment for the service rendered. The most common provision prohibits any kind of payment to a trustee but allows reimbursement of out-of-pocket expenses.

The board or trustee have a special authority to hold executive meetings outside of the annual meeting in order to act in the best interests of the members.

FAILURE TO PAY MORTGAGE, MONTHLY MAINTENANCE FEE

Mortgage default is a scenario in which the borrower does not make payment on the mortgage and the loan is deemed as "in default" meaning that the lender gets the right to take over the property. Defaulting on a mortgage can lead to loss of a valuable chunk of real estate and must be avoided under any circumstances. Even if the lender does not take over the property, a mortgage default can significantly pull down a credit score making it difficult to negotiate with financial institutions or secure credit from lenders in the future. A monthly payments due date is specified along with the issuance of a mortgage. A grace period (delay) of one to two weeks is allowed for making payments. After this late fees become applicable. If more than 30 days pass by after the due date, then the mortgage is said to be in default. A default notice is issued after 60 to 90 days, which is the first step to foreclosure proceedings and disposal for the property by the lender through an auction.

Some mortgagees deliberately default on their mortgages and just walk away, preferring the negative impact on their credit score than putting more equity into their property. At the first sign of mortgage default risk the property owner should contact the lender to negotiate. Most lenders are sensitive to mortgagees' woes and offer to help in terms of extending the grace period or accepting reduced payments

If paying mortgage dues is a problem for property owners then defaulting on payment of condominium monthly maintenance charges is a definite logical possibility. Condominium boards have the right and are encouraged to proactively collect late fees from defaulting condo unit owners. Condo boards must track 'aging reports' closely that indicate the average time required to collect regular maintenance and capital expenditure dues from condo members. Condo boards do not have any means to know if a unit owner is defaulting on mortgage payments. The 6(d) certificate, to be issued by the Board of Trustees, lists all the fees, fines and other dues payable to the condo association by the unit owner or the mortgage company in the case of a foreclosure or re-financing.

Failure to pay the monthly maintenance fee will result in a lien being attached to the defaulting condominium unit and the possibility of foreclosure proceedings being initiated. Collection of late payment fees involves a legal process and it has to be done in accordance with the federal Fair Debt Collection Practices Act, 1966. This act specifies certain rights that indebted individuals possess.

In Massachusetts, the condominium statute includes a provision for "super lien" (M.G.L. c.400, § 183A) that empowers the association to become the first lien holder on a property on the verge of default. In a typical scenario, when a unit owner is late by 30 – 45 days in payment of condominium maintenance fees, a demand letter is sent that provides details of the debt situation and highlights the people's right as per the FDCPA. If no response is received in another 30 days from such a demand letter, notices are issued to the unit owner and the first mortgage holder that include a 60-days late warning. Another separate notice is issued to the first mortgage holder warning about a suit to be filed in the court by the association, if unpaid fees remain unpaid up to 30 days. In Massachusetts, when such a complaint is filed, the "super lien" becomes applicable. Associations are required to act quickly to retain their 'super lien' status with respect to the original owner. Mortgage lenders initiating an auction or foreclosure proceedings against a unit owner are required to give only a three weeks' notice to the condo association. Hence the opportunity for collecting pending dues may simply wither away. Associations are interested in just recovering the fees due and not own the condo unit through foreclosure. In most cases, the threat of a super lien to the unit owner or the mortgage lender is sufficient to make them pay the pending dues.

Whenever a condo unit owner defaults on maintenance fees, the other unit owners together bear the defaulter's expenses and that is unfair. If the fee payment default exceeds 60 days, then foreclosure proceedings must be initiated through a lawyer. While the board members feel sympathetic towards the unit holder, the best interests of the entire community have to be foremost. Foreclosure proceedings must start on schedule in order to preserve the priority lien that the association gains as per the Massachusetts law. This law only protects the association's right to the fees due within six months prior to the foreclosure filing. Longer the delay in initiating foreclosure, lesser is the protection from the law.

CLOSING DOCUMENTS--6D CERTIFICATE, INSURANCE CERTIFICATE

6(d) Certificate

This is an itemized statement provided by the condominium association of owners listing the break-up of charges due to be paid by the unit owner to the association. This statement is defined in and references section 6(d) of M.G.L. c. 183A, hence the name 6(d) certificate.

For a condominium buyer, this certificate is a critical disclosure, which is required to be provided by the owners' association within 10 business days following a written request and payment of requisite fees. The certificate contents are binding on the condominium owners' association and prohibit it from enforcing a lien for recovering any expenses that were due before the date of the 6(d) certificate and not mentioned in it.

The seller, seller's agent or any representative are required to procure the 6(d) certificate, as commonly done, preceding a closing. In case of a mortgage foreclosure, the mortgagee is not required to pay any fee for obtaining the 6(d) certificate.

At closing, the 6(d) certificate certifies that there are no outstanding assessments or condo fees for the unit.

NOTE: For new condo developments, an offer to purchase or preliminary agreement should be subject to review of the bylaws and subject to refund of deposit.

Insurance Certificate

Condominium associations are required to procure a master hazard and liability insurance policy that covers all the common areas and specific installed parts of each individual unit. Such a master insurance certificate does not cover the personal property or enhancements of individual units. The individual unit owners must independently insure their personal belongings, personal liability and enhancements within their respective units through a separate insurance policy / certificate. Note: Unit owners may be responsible for property damage and personal injury to others as a result of their negligence. For enhanced coverage, unit owners purchase casualty insurance for protection against personal injury and property claims and a fire and theft policy for personal belongings inside the unit.

DISADVANTAGES OF CONDOMINIUMS

The primary disadvantage to condo ownership applies to small and large developments. In small associations (1-4 units), unit owners can be affected by the non-payment of fees by one unit owner. The fees that are used to cover the master insurance, common utilities and maintenance are hampered when one or more unit owners fall behind.

In larger condo developments, the condo board may agree to make changes or improvements to the building and the cost will then be distributed among all of the unit owners. This is sometimes referred to as a *special assessment.* Special assessments are generally not due all at once. Payments are added to the normal condo fees over a period of 12-36 months.

MASSACHUSETTS CONDO CONVERSION

Massachusetts Condominium Conversion Statute, Chapter 527 of the Acts of 1983

Major Conversion Provisions- Applies to co-ops as well as condos; doesn't apply to buildings containing less than 4 residential units-Review highlights of the law, including tenants have a period of time to purchase on terms and conditions the same or more favorable than those extended to the general public.

A written notice is required of an owner's intent to convert a building as well as an explanation of tenants' rights.

Protected Classes

a. Elderly, Handicapped, Low or Moderate Income - 62 years+. Physically handicapped, income less than 80% of median income for the area set forth in HUD regulations.

A tenant is protected if there is merely an intent to convert. For example: a Master Deed is prepared, Purchase and Sale Agreements are prepared, there are inspections, measurements, surveys, showings, advertising, etc.

Buildings of less than four (4) residential units are exempt. In determining whether the four (4) units minimum is met, units in two (2) adjacent buildings with common ownership will be added together.

b. A limit on rent increases: CPI or ten percent (10%), whichever is greater.

c. Time to Vacate- 1 year for elderly, disabled and low to moderate income people.;

These protected classes have two (2) years or longer (up to two (2) more years) if they cannot find comparable rental housing in the same City or Town.

The Boston ordinance gives elderly, handicapped and low income tenants five (5) years but says that the notice period may be extended by future legislation. This could mean that a tenant in a protected class in Boston could conceivably be protected indefinitely.

d. Moving reimbursement -Up to $750.00 of documented expenses for non-protected classes; up to $1,000 for protected classes. Tenant has to be up-to-date on rent payments and voluntarily vacate before end of notice period to be eligible for reimbursement.

e. Tenant's right to purchase: a tenant has a ninety (90) day period to purchase on the same terms as or more favorable terms as those which will be extended to the general public. I have had tenants execute a waiver of the tenant's right to purchase a rental unit. The tenant, in the waiver, acknowledges that he received a purchase and sale agreement executed by the owner of the apartment building and that he was notified that the terms and conditions of the agreement were substantially the same as or more favorable than the terms and conditions which will be offered to the general public during the ninety (90) day purchase period.

f. Penalties: Fine of not less than one thousand dollars $1,000) or imprisonment of not less than sixty (60) days.

Chapter 527 prohibits evictions for the purpose of converting a building to condominiums. However, a tenant may be evicted for any violation of the lease, including non-payment of rent, provided that this is not merely a pretext for a condominium conversion eviction.

**Any city or town may impose their own conversion regulations in lieu of this statute (Use example such as recent adoption of condominium conversion ordinance by city of Boston).

The timing of property ownership recordings can create confusion in many instances, especially when a property has been converted into a condominium. For every condominium created there will be a window of time when the condo unit owners are not each receiving their own Individualized tax bill. **This DOES NOT mean that each condo owner is not responsible for property taxes.**

COOPERATIVES (VS CONDOMINIUMS)

(M.G.L. c. 157B)

Co-op owners are occupants and do not own their units. They buy a share in the co-op association. Occupants purchase stock shares which entitle each occupant to a long-term lease of one of the apartment units.

On reading this section completely, you will understand;

- What is a stock certificate in corporation?
- What is a proprietary unit lease?
- What blanket mortgage means?
- How cooperatives are taxed?

STOCK CERTIFICATE IN CORPORATION

Cooperatives are individual units in a multi-unit apartment complex. Although conceptually similar to condominiums, they differ significantly with respect to ownership, title and funding aspects.

In Massachusetts, only a cooperative corporation (partnership or trust) has the authority to construct, acquire, or convert an apartment building to cooperative ownership and it is mandatory to include the word 'cooperative' in the name of every cooperative corporation. Such a corporation sells shares (stock) similar to any other corporation. The purchaser of stock interest in a cooperative corporation is issued a stock certificate.

PROPRIETARY UNIT LEASE FOR LIFE OF CORPORATION

The stock purchased in a cooperative corporation is accompanied by a proprietary lease to one dwelling unit in the constructed building. Thus the stockholder becomes the owner of a unit in the building constructed by the cooperative corporation.

This proprietary lease gets automatically transferred with the stock.

Selling a co-op unit

If the stockholder later sells or transfers their stock. The stockholders interest can be sold or transferred as long as the sale is within the rules set forth in the bylaws. Many sales of co-op shares are subject to the right of first refusal and/or the approval of the board. The proprietary unit lease remains with that cooperative corporation for life and simply gets transferred to new owners within the same corporation.

CO-OP MONTHLY FEES

Stockholders pay a monthly fee which generally includes real estate taxes, insurance, maintenance, and a proportionate amount of principal and interest.

CORPORATION OBTAINS BLANKET MORTGAGE

The corporation obtains a blanket mortgage loan, which is secured by the whole building, under the same financing terms as mortgage of real property.

Stockholders owning proprietary leases share a single mortgage loan obtained by the corporation.

TAXED AS ONE ENTITY

The cooperative corporation is provided only a single real estate tax bill by the Massachusetts governing authorities, which is shared by the stockholders with proprietary leases along with the maintenance costs.

BOARD OF DIRECTORS

The residents elect a Board of Directors that manages the cooperative. The Board of Directors are the governing body and makes management decisions.

DISADVANTAGE OF COOPERATIVES

- Single mortgage

- One tax bill

Higher risks to shareholders in case of co-op owner default on payment - the difference need to be made up by other shareholders. The bank financing co-op loans is in second position to the bank holding mortgages on the building. The Board establishes the amount of financing allowable for unsubsidized market rate cooperatives, more limited availability of co-op financing, because the only collateral is the lease and the stock certificates.

Condominium vs. Cooperative Comparison

	Condominium	Cooperative
Purchasing process	Unit mortgage	Co-op loan
How interest is conveyed?	Deed	Stock transfer
Can unit be mortgaged?	Yes	No
Can building be mortgaged?	No	Yes
Owners rights	Fee Simple Deed	Proprietary Lease
Units taxed separately	Yes	No
Ownership restriction	No	Yes*
Transferability	Yes	Possible financing issues
Real estate taxes/mortgage interest tax deductible	Yes	Yes

*Cooperatives may impose transfer restrictions (including right of first refusal) as long as they do not violate laws against discrimination.

(M.G.L c. 183B)

On reading this section completely, you will understand;

- The definition of weekly ownership of timeshares.
- The role of exchange organizations.
- The maintenance and management fees associated with timeshares.
- Ways of acquiring timeshares.

DEFINITION - WEEKLY OWNERSHIP (INTERVAL OWNERSHIP)

A time-share unit is an attached condominium or converted hotel/motel rooms.

A time-share is a type of joint-ownership of real property that is similar in concept to condominiums but with the applicability of time limits. A large number of owners or lessees share the costs of owning the property and occupancy rights (usually for a week at a stretch) during multiple time periods (weekly) separated by gaps, as per a specific schedule (generally yearly).

Massachusetts laws consider time-shares as real estate.

EXCHANGE ORGANIZATION

Exchange is significant part of the timeshare offer. It has played a major role in popularizing the timeshare concept. An exchange program is one that permits the assignment or exchange of rights for timeshare occupancy among timeshare owners within the same or different timeshare properties.

Exchange organizations operate as brokers between various timeshare owners. They offer timeshare owners the opportunity to exchange their timeshare for one week at a different resort with the assurance of experiencing similar quality.

The three leading exchange organizations are Resort Condominiums International (RCI), Trading Places International (TPI), and Interval International (II). Together they incorporate about 5400 resorts in timeshare programs. Mostly all timeshare resorts have membership of either of these organizations. In cases where the resort is affiliated, the timeshare owner becomes part of the exchange organization during purchase.

Exchange organizations operate like banks. If a timeshare owner does not wish to utilize the 'week' or 'resort' purchased, he or she can deposit it with the exchange organization. They can later withdraw an equivalent week at another resort deposited by other owners. Exchange organizations possess mechanisms for matching properties depending on a multitude of factors that help ascertain the value of different weeks in various resorts. Factors such as property size, time of year, period of stay, resort quality and location are considered to assess the relative value of the properties available. Exchange organizations use a point system, similar to currencies, to derive the relative value of the weeks.

- Resort Condominiums International http://www.rci.com/

- Trading Spaces International http://tradingspaces.com

- Interval International http://www.intervalworld.com/

MAINTENANCE AND MANAGEMENT FEES

In addition to the initial cost of purchasing a timeshare, each timeshare owner is charged an annual maintenance fee to cover the costs of staffing, common expenses, operations and maintenance of the resort. A part of the maintenance fee is deposited in to a reserve fund to account for major repairs or improvements to be carried out as and when necessary. The money to be deposited into the reserve fund is calculated on the basis of a reserve study conducted to estimate the life of major elements such as swimming pool, climate-control system, roof, appliances, parking-lot pavements, carpets, furnishings etc. and anticipate redecoration as per a defined schedule. The resort's documents provide an estimation of the maintenance fee, highlight the reserve-study results and detail the reserve-fund allocation.

A 'special assessment' is a one-time fee charged to every timeshare owner. For example, $500 may be charged to each timeshare owner to cover the cost of a new roof that was not provisioned for in the reserve fund by the board of directors of the timeshare resort. This may also be used to fund improvements that were not thought of and included in the reserve-study such as an additional parking-lot or a recreational facility.

Every timeshare resort is levied a 'property tax' as it is considered as a real estate, similar to a house or a residential condominium. A portion of such property tax is proportionately charged to each timeshare owner and is included in the annual bill along with the maintenance fee

Some timeshare resorts may charge separate fees for 'recreation, activity and service' that can significantly hike the vacationing costs for residing owners. Additional rental fees may be charged for water sports equipment, beach chairs and cabanas, tennis courts and videos etc.

Other typical fee-based activities may include golf, skiing, horse-riding and scuba-diving etc. for which owners may be offered preferential rates.

An admission fee may be charged to owners and guests for picnics, receptions and such other functions to cover some of the additional costs, although most of the costs are covered in the annual maintenance fees.

Mid-week housekeeping services may be offered to all resort occupants as an amenity or provided for an additional fee to those who wish to avail it.

Telephone facility may be offered free or charged per-call, even for long-distance or toll-free numbers.

OWNERSHIP VS RIGHT TO USE

(M.G.L. c. 183B, §3)

Owners buy an undivided interest in a unit with an additional right to use facilities for a specific time period.

In Massachusetts, interest in a time-share (time-share estate) can be acquired in two possible ways;

1. Ownership through a deed (fee-simple estate) in a unit offering the right of possession spanning a possibly unlimited number of time periods (one week at a stretch) separated by pre-determined gaps between two such time periods.

2. Right to Use (estate for years) through a grant in a unit bestowing the right of possession spanning five or more distinctly separated time periods during a specified number of years (five or more) that include options to extend or renew.

LEASES AND OPTIONS

On reading this section completely, you will understand;

- What are freehold and non-freehold properties?
- The meaning of Lessor, Lessee, Term, Lease and Demised.

FREEHOLD VS NON-FREEHOLD

Freehold and Non-Freehold (a.k.a. Leasehold), both, are types of property that are developed according to the common law system. Freehold estates can be held forever or until the possessor is alive. Non-Freehold or Leasehold estates can be held for a fixed time period as per the calendar. Although, freehold and non-freehold property are differentiated by the time duration of their respective possession, both are deemed as present possessory estates.

This topic is covered in more detail in Chapter I of this book.

LESSOR, LESSEE, TERM, LEASE, DEMISED

Lessor

This is the term used to refer to a landlord in a rental agreement. Landlord is the owner of the property, in this case the condominium. Thus, the lessor is the owner of the condominium here.

Lessee

This is the term used to refer to the tenant in a rental agreement. Tenant is the person who takes the property on rental basis, in this case the condominium. Thus, the lessee is the renter of the condominium here.

Term

This is the duration for which a rental agreement remains in force. In other words, it is the time period for which the lessor gives out the property on rent to the lessee. This is agreed between the two parties and mentioned in the rental agreement.

Lease

The rental agreement between the lessor and the lessee is termed as a Lease. This agreement lists all the details of the lessor and lessee as well as all the terms and conditions of the rental deal.

Demised

In case of commercial lease, the space that the tenant wishes to lease is called the 'demised premises'. In other words, the 'leased' premise is known as the 'demised' premise. The lease must clearly define and mention the demised premises and the tenant must ensure that the demised premises that he or expects to receive is the same as the demised premises defined in the lease agreement.

Certain words (demise) must be used in a lease;

- Leases to---

- Does hereby let and demise—

Demise is a conveyance of use.

A written lease is not required by Massachusetts law. Tenants without leases still have rights.

A lease is a contract and is subject to the same requirements of other contracts. At a minimum: consideration, offer and acceptance, legal capacity of the parties and signatures are required. While details will vary from state to state, leases should contain the following essential information regardless of location:

Competent Parties Both the landlord and tenant must be of legal age. In most states, 18 years of age is known as "majority" and therefore of legal age. States recognize that a person aged less than 18 years of age ("infancy") to legally own real property, but they may not allow such a person to enter into a contract concerning that property.

All parties must be able to understand ALL the terms of the contract. "Being of sound mind" is a legal phrase that describes the ability of a person to comprehend the nature, extent, and consequences of his or her decisions. Mentally ill or incapacitated persons, as well as felons serving a prison sentence, are generally considered legally incompetent and are excluded from entering into lease agreements or other legal contracts.

Legal Purpose The intent and purpose of the agreement must be allowed under state and local law. A valid lease agreement may not contain terms or conditions that are illegal.

Statute of Frauds The phrase "statute of frauds" does not apply to any specific piece of legislation. Rather, it refers to the legal concept that certain kinds of contracts, including real estate contracts, must be in writing to be considered valid and enforceable. In Massachusetts, all leases must be in writing to be enforceable.

Reversionary Right There isn't a specific time frame that a lease must be for. A lease agreement can vary, depending on what type of leasehold estate was initially granted to the tenant (see Leasehold Estates). The lease agreement must show that possession and ownership of the premises reverts to the landlord at the end of the lease.

Property Description The real property to be leased must be named and described in the lease agreement itself. Generally, the street address is sufficient, especially for residential leases. One exception may be, a long-term lease, such as a net lease, ground lease, or shell lease, which should always contain the legal description.

Mutual Assent (Offer and Acceptance) This is a requirement of most contracts. One party (the "offeror") must make an offer to another party (the "offeree"). The terms and conditions of the contract must be amenable and acceptable to both parties. In a lease agreement, the offeror (landlord) promises to allow the offeree (tenant) to possess, use, and occupy the premises according to certain rules and conditions, in return for some sort of consideration, which usually take the form of rent payments. Possession of the property by the tenant implies acceptance of the offer.

Consideration The landlord receives rental payments from the tenant in return for the use and possession of the landlord's property. *Example: On farms, non-monetary consideration may be provided (labor or crops).*

Let and Demise A statement of intent to "let and demise" is a proclamation by the landlord that he or she intends to let (lease or rent) the premises to the tenant exclusively. The term demise means to convey an estate by lease. Without this statement, the tenant has no legal interest in the real property. This means that a leasehold estate has not been created and therefore the lease agreement is not valid.

Duration of Occupancy Lease agreements should contain a statement describing the duration of the lease. Leases can be from 1 week to several years. The exception would be an *estate at will*, which allows the tenant to possess the property for an indefinite and unspecified period of time.

Signatures The lease must be signed by all parties and delivered to the tenant. It is not required that leases are notarized unless it is to be recorded.

Special Lease Issues

Recording of leases is not essential. There is a seven-year rule in Massachusetts. A lease of seven years or more is not binding on a new owner unless the notice of a lease is recorded (constructive notice), or the buyer has actual notice of the lease.

TYPES OF TENANCY

On reading this section completely, you will understand;

- What is tenancy for years?
- What is tenancy from period to period?
- What is the meaning of tenancy at Will?
- What does tenancy at sufferance mean?

ESTATE/TENANCY FOR YEARS

The unique characteristic of a tenancy-for-years lease is that it starts and ends on a particular date. For example, a lease that starts on April 1 and ends on December 31, nine months later, is an estate-for-years. Neither party involved is required to issue a notice for terminating such kind of a lease. Such a lease expires when the defined lease term ends.

In such a lease, the lessee (tenant) agrees to pay rental charges for each month over the term of the lease. In the event that the tenant moves out of the rented premises before the lease term ends, without the landlord's permission, then the tenant is liable to pay the entire pending balance amount of the lease. In such a situation, the landlord is required to make reasonable efforts to search and acquire a new tenant to compensate the balance amount of the former tenant's lease. This is termed as the landlord's duty towards damage mitigation.

A lease can be for a period of time from one day to 99 years.

ESTATE/TENANCY FROM PERIOD TO PERIOD

A tenancy from period to period continues for a length of time that it is not certain. An amount of rent is payable at definite intervals. Example: the rent for 6 months is $6000.00. The tenancy will extend every six months regardless if the rent is paid monthly or semi-annually. Either party must give six months notice to terminate.

The reservation of rent distinguishes period to period from tenancy at will. Tenancy at will would require a 30 day notice.

ESTATE/TENANCY AT WILL

Tenancy at will is created when the landlord accepts rent and gives the tenant a key to the unit. All the tenancy terms and conditions continue to apply indefinitely till the time that either of the parties involved issues an appropriate termination. Such a notice comes into effect on the subsequent due date of rent payment following a 30-day period of advance notice. The minimum mandatory notice period is 30 days. In the case of rooming houses, where the rent becomes due on a weekly or daily basis, the notice period applicable is seven days. In Massachusetts, a minimum 30 day notice is required regardless of rental period.

Tenancy is terminated upon the death of the tenant, but not by death of the landlord.

ESTATE/TENANCY AT SUFFERANCE

(M.G.L. c. 186, § 3)

Tenancy at sufferance is created when a tenant remains in possession of a property after the tenancy has been legally terminated. The landlord may recover payments for use of the property while in sufferance. Note: If the landlord accepts any payment before the tenant in sufferance leaves, a tenancy at will is now created.

Hold over tenant – while similar to tenancy at sufferance, a hold over tenant is one whose lease has expired and they remain in possession of the property. They have the same rights as a tenant at sufferance.

COMMON LEASES

On reading this section completely, you will understand;

- What is Gross Lease and Modified Gross Lease?
- Net Lease and its variations.
- What is a Percentage Lease?
- The meaning of Graduated Lease.
- Special lease issues are addressed.
- 7 Year rule

GROSS, NET (INCL. TRIPLE NET EX.), PERCENTAGE, GRADUATED

Leases are generally classified on the basis of what the tenant is required to pay or the options that the tenant has.

Gross Lease

Most residential leases fall under this category, where the landlord bears majority of the expenses incurred, such as water, sewage, taxes and insurance linked to the property while the tenant is required to pay the rent and bear the expenses that vary significantly depending on the extent of use by the tenant, such as electricity and heat. This is because excess utility consumption beyond the standards of the building has to be paid by the tenant. Hence the tenant must clarify which utilities and janitorial services are offered and their frequency.

This type of lease is beneficial for the tenant as it provides for a single tenant-friendly rent payment making it easy to forecast expenses without bothering much about charges. The responsibility of the entire building rests with the landlord, while the tenants can focus on their business.

Net Leases

This type of lease is popular among commercial tenants, where the tenant is charged a lower base rent but is required to pay majority of the property expenses associated with operations, maintenance and use such as taxes, insurance, property management fees, common area maintenance (CAM) including janitorial services, parking, landscaping, sewer, water, fire sprinklers, trash collection and such other common services.

Net leases are of several types such as;

Single Net Lease (Net or N)

In this type of lease, the tenant pays a base rent and an additional pro-rata share of the property tax of the building i.e. a part of the total bill, which is proportional to the total building area leased by the tenant. The landlord pays all other expenses incurred. The tenant also bears the utilities and janitorial service charges.

Double Net Lease (Net-Net or NN)

Here, the tenant is required to pay a base rent and an additional pro-rata share of the property taxes as well as insurance. The landlord bears the expenses incurred for structural repairs and maintaining the common areas. The tenant also has to bear the utility and janitorial expenses.

Triple Net Lease (Net-Net-Net or NNN)

This is a very popular type of net lease commonly found in commercial buildings and retail deals. This type of lease requires the tenant to pay the entire or a part of the three 'nets' – property taxes, insurance and common area maintenance – in addition to a base monthly rent. Common area utilities and maintenance is usually included as well. For example, the cost of employing a lobby attendant is included in the NNN fees. Tenants also have to pay their own occupancy costs, including utilities and janitorial services as well as insurance and taxes.

Landlords usually draw an estimate of the expenses to be incurred and charge a part of such estimated expenses on a proportionate or pro-rata basis. For example, a tenant leasing 1000 square feet of a 10000 square feet property has to pay 10% of the property's taxes, insurance and CAM.

Triple net leases are more landlord-friendly; hence tenants must carefully scrutinize NNN charges and negotiate ceilings on the amounts, as they can be increased annually. An NNN lease may differ across months or years as operational expenses may fluctuate higher or lower, rendering the business' expense forecasting tricky and inaccurate.

But NNN leases include tenant benefits too. Transparency is one of these, as tenants can view the business operating expenses against the charges that they pay. Cost savings in operational expenses are credited to the tenant's account instead of the landlord's. Further, in an NNN lease the monthly rent is potentially lower compared to a gross lease as tenants bear a greater responsibility for the building.

Absolute Triple Net Lease

A less common type of lease, it has greater binding and rigidity than the NNN lease. In this lease, the tenants bear every possible real estate risk such as responsibility for construction expenses i.e. rebuilding following a disaster; continuing rent payment even after condemnation of the building etc. Tenants bear ultimate responsibility for the property under ALL circumstances.

Modified Gross Lease

This type of lease is a kind of compromise between the gross lease, which is more tenant-friendly, and the net lease, which is more landlord-friendly. Also known as the 'modified net lease', this lease is similar to a gross lease as the rent is paid / collected in a lump sum amount and may include any or all of the 'nets' such as property taxes, insurance and common area maintenance (CAM). Utilities and janitorial services are usually excluded from the rent and have to be borne by the tenant separately. Tenants and landlords may negotiate about which of the 'nets' should be included in the base rental amount.

The modified gross lease is quite popular with tenants as it flexibility leads to a simpler landlord-tenant agreement. In this lease, unlike the NNN lease, the lease rate remains unchanged even in the event of an increase in taxes, insurance or CAM. However, in case of decrease in these expenses, the landlord gets the benefit. Since electricity and janitorial services are not included, tenants retain better control over their spends in this lease as compared to a gross lease.

Percentage Lease

Another type of commercial lease that is commonly associated with retail properties is the Percentage lease. Here the tenant pays a pre-determined minimum rent amount and in addition, a percentage of his or her monthly income that exceeds a specified amount. For example the tenant has to pay $1500 per month as a fixed rent and in addition 10% of gross income over $300000. The percentage lease is frequently used in the retail business due to its significant seasonal variation characteristic. This enables retailers to minimize their expenses in times of lower income. The landlord reserves the right to audit the tenants records periodically.

Graduated Lease

Also referred to as a step-up lease. Other increases may be tied to the Consumer Price Index (CPI). This is another type of variable lease that results in variable rent amount. Here the rent is increased on stipulated dates, say every three months or four months. Such dates and agreed terms are included in the lease agreement. This is beneficial for both the tenant and the landlord as the rent is increased gradually. The tenant is especially benefitted if he or she has difficulty in paying a large rent amount initially but expects the situation to improve over a period of time.

SPECIAL LEASES

Special leases are required when an arrangement can be advantageous to one or both parties.

Sale and Leaseback

Sale and leaseback is a form of financing wherein the owner sells a property generally to obtain working capital and in turn leases the property from the new owner. Another form of leaseback is for the owner to erect a building on a property and sells the building and property to a prearranged buyer and leases it back to the seller.

The advantage is that the new tenant may now deduct the rent as a business expense.

Ground Lease

Land is leased to a tenant who agrees to build a structure on it. The lease requires the tenant to pay ground rent, insurance, real estate taxes, and maintenance. Ground leases are generally written for a minimum of fifty years. The leaseholder has the right to sell the structure or improvement and assign the ground lease to the buyer.

Reappraisal Lease

Provides for rent increases based on independent appraisals.

ESSENTIAL LEASE REQUIREMENTS

A lease is a contract and is subject to the same requirements of other contracts. At a minimum: consideration, offer and acceptance, legal capacity of the parties and signatures are required. While details will vary from state to state, leases should contain the following essential information regardless of location:

Competent Parties Both the landlord and tenant must be of legal age. In most states, 18 years of age is known as "majority" and therefore of legal age. States recognize that a person aged less than 18 years of age ("infancy") to legally own real property, but they may not allow such a person to enter into a contract concerning that property.

All parties must be able to understand ALL the terms of the contract. "Being of sound mind" is a legal phrase that describes the ability of a person to comprehend the nature, extent, and consequences of his or her decisions. Mentally ill or incapacitated persons, as well as felons serving a prison sentence, are generally considered legally incompetent and are excluded from entering into lease agreements or other legal contracts.

Legal Purpose The intent and purpose of the agreement must be allowed under state and local law. A valid lease agreement may not contain terms or conditions that are illegal.

Statute of Frauds The phrase "statute of frauds" does not apply to any specific piece of legislation. Rather, it refers to the legal concept that certain kinds of contracts, including real estate contracts, must be in writing to be considered valid and enforceable. In Massachusetts, all leases must be in writing to be enforceable.

Term of the Lease The lease must contain a definite period of time. Long-term leases are not written for more than ninety-nine years.

Description of Premises The real property to be leased must be named and described in the lease agreement itself. Generally, the street address including all appurtenances (parking, basement and storage space). One exception may be, a long-term lease, such as a net lease, ground lease, or shell lease, which should always contain the legal description.

Mutual Assent (Offer and Acceptance) This is a requirement of most contracts. One party (the "offeror") must make an offer to another party (the "offeree"). The terms and conditions of the contract must be amenable and acceptable to both parties. In a lease agreement, the offeror (landlord) promises to allow the offeree (tenant) to possess, use, and occupy the premises according to certain rules and conditions, in return for some sort of consideration, which usually take the form of rent payments. Possession of the property by the tenant implies acceptance of the offer.

Consideration The landlord must include the total rent for the entire term of the lease and identify the amount and time of periodic payments.

Let and Demise A statement of intent to "let and demise" is a proclamation by the landlord that he or she intends to let (lease or rent) the premises to the tenant exclusively. The term demise means to convey an estate by lease. Without this statement, the tenant has no legal interest in the real property. This means that a leasehold estate has not been created and therefore the lease agreement is not valid.

Signatures The lease must be signed by all parties and delivered to the tenant. It is not required that leases are notarized unless it is to be recorded.

7 YEAR RULE

Recording of leases is not essential. There is a seven-year rule in Massachusetts. A lease of seven years or more is not binding on a new owner unless the notice of a lease is recorded (constructive notice), or the buyer has actual notice of the lease.

COVENANTS IN LEASES

EXPRESSED

Express covenants are agreed upon between the landlord and the tenant. In a written lease, the wording of intent of exactly what to do or what not to do makes an expressed covenant. Expressed covenants are meant to protect both the landlord's rights as well as the tenant's rights.

Use of Premises

Restrictions on use of the property is set forth in the lease. For residential leases, it is assumed that the tenant will be living there. A restriction may include not renting out rooms or participating in any illegal activity. Commercial leases may restrict the leased space to a type of business (i.e. no restaurants or convenience stores).

Security Deposits

Monies are generally secured in cases where the tenant may cause damage to a property. State law regulates the handling of security deposits.

Number of Persons to Occupy

Leases may limit the number of persons that are allowed in a unit. Landlords may terminate leases if tenants are found in violation of this covenant with the exception of a tenant adopting a child or having a baby.

Insurance Requirement

Residential and commercial tenants should maintain hazard or rental insurance in cases where losses are due to the tenants' negligence. In commercial leases, hazard insurance is often required. Residential tenants should note that in some situations where the loss is not due to the fault of the tenant, the landlord's insurance will not cover any losses beyond *loss of use*.

Assignment and Subleasing

Most leases expressly prohibit assignment and subleasing without the approval of the landlord. Subleasing transfers the usage of a premises, and the liability remains with the original lessee. In an assignment, the assignee becomes directly liable to the landlord for the rent. Subleasing or assignment may be appropriate in instances where the lessee is not able to complete the lease due to work or hardship and has found a replacement suitable to the landlord.

Rent Adjustments

An increase or decrease in the yearly rent can be based on the Consumer Price Index (CPI) or the number of occupants. (i.e. $500 increase for each additional persons over 4).

Restrictive Covenants

Includes items that are generally in the use of premises as well as issues that may affect other tenants (parties after 9pm, pets, excessive noise, changing of locks, installing antennas from cable companies, mounting signs on the building etc.).

Obligation to Make Repairs

The law requires landlords to keep the premises in a safe and habitable condition. Lease conditions that conflict with state statutes are not enforceable. In some commercials leases, the tenant may be required to maintain the heating system.

Improvements to the Premises

Improvements to leases properties should be agreed to in advance and included within the lease. Any improvements will generally become the property of the landlord unless there is an agreement for removal. Trade fixtures are generally removed from the premises after lease termination.

Option to Renew

An option to renew gives the tenant an opportunity to renew (sign a new lease) for an additional term when both parties can agree upon specified conditions.

Option to Purchase

An option to purchase gives the tenant the opportunity to purchase with property within a specified period of time and with specific terms that are already agreed upon.

Right of First Refusal

This gives the tenant the right to purchases the property at equal terms that has been offered to the public. In some cases, the right to renew the lease if the property is sold may be included in the lease agreement.

Automatic Extension Clause

Automatic lease extension is generally included in residential lease agreements. The lease extends automatically unless the landlord or the tenant gives prior notice.

Tax Escalation Clause

This clause allows the landlord to adjust the rent based on an increase in the annual real estate taxes.

IMPLIED

Implied covenants are inferred and implied by law. Landlord and tenant imply certain duties and obligations to effect the purposes on which the contract is made.

Quiet Enjoyment

The right of the tenant to use the property without any disturbance or interference from the landlord.

Prevention of Waste

At all times, the tenant is expected to keep the property clean and free of debris or any items that may diminish the property value. Normal wear and tear is not a violation of this implied covenant.

TERMINATION OF TENANCIES AND LEASES

The basic laws governing the notice to quit can be found in M.G.L. c. 186 § 11; 12. The notice must be timely, definite, unequivocal, and stated with particularity, so that it can be reasonably understood.

Leases may be terminated for the following:

- Mutual agreement

- Expiration of the lease

- Proper notice (by either party)

- Condemnation

- Destruction

- Abandonment

- Breach of leasing terms

- Mortgage foreclosure

TERMINATION

14-day Notice

There are two types of Notices to Quit. The first type is called a 14-Day Notice to Quit. A 14-Day Notice to Quit is only used when a tenant does not pay his or her rent. If a tenant receives this type of Notice to Quit, he or she can "cure" by paying the full amount of the rent owed within 10 days of receiving the notice.

30-day Notice

The second type of Notice to Quit is called a 30-Day Notice to Quit. A 30-Day Notice to Quit can list any reason for eviction, other than non-payment of rent, or no reason for eviction in a situation where the tenant is considered a tenant-at-will. In order to be valid, a 30-Day Notice to Quit must be received at least 30 days, or one full rental period, in advance of the "deliver up" date.

Constructive Eviction

This type of conviction is complete when the actions of the landlord prevent the tenant from enjoyment and use of the premises and the tenant moves out. This type of eviction is generally illegal.

Death

Death of the landlord or the tenant does not terminate a lease. The obligation is binding on the estates of either person.

Note: (1) In Massachusetts, if a mobile home park tenant dies, the lease continues for a further year from the date of the death of the primary tenant. (2) A tenancy at will terminate upon the death of the tenant or the landlord.

Sale of the Premises

A sale does not terminate a lease. Tenants are allowed to stay until their lease ends. In order to stay, a new lease must be signed with the new owner. Regarding commercial leases for seven years or more, the lease is binding upon the new landlord if the lease is recorded in the registry of deeds (constructive notice) or the prospective owner is notified of the lease before the sale (actual notice).

On reading this section completely, you will understand;

- What are Utilities in a multi-unit apartment or condominium?
- The habitability requirements and the State Sanitary Code.
- What constitute Sanitary and Building Codes violations?
- How to avoid waste when residing in a multi-unit building or condo?
- All about security deposit.

UTILITIES (M.G.L. c. 25; 220 CMR)

Utilities are amenities or facilities that are provided to each unit in a multi-unit building or condominium such as water, electricity, gas, heat, cable, phone and waste disposal etc. Each utility is usually metered separately and is provided and managed by different utility companies. Utilities are charged to the tenant as per consumption typically on a monthly basis. Hence utility charges vary according to use and they may be charged separately or included in the rent by the landlord. Which of the utilities will be charged and who is responsible for the payment has to be clearly specified in the lease agreement between the landlord and the tenant or the condominium association documents, as relevant.

FIT FOR HABITATION (105 CMR 410)

The Massachusetts Department of Public Health stipulates rules detailing the standards that occupants and property owners must maintain. Such regulations safeguard the health, safety and welfare of Massachusetts citizens and are enumerated in the chapter II of the State Sanitary Code (105 CMR 410) under the title 'Minimum Standards of Fitness for Human Habitation'.

The Massachusetts State Sanitary Code specifies a number of benchmarks and requirements applicable to all dwelling units for maintaining minimum standards of habitability. These standards are applicable to each owner-occupied or rented residential unit or dwelling unit or mobile dwelling unit or rooming house unit that is used for the purpose of living, eating, cooking and sleeping in Massachusetts. Dwelling unit also includes condominium unit. These rules are legally enforceable and the primary responsibility rests with local health boards.

Some of the key standards specified in the State Sanitary Code are;

Number of Occupants

The state sanitary code specifies the maximum number of occupants permitted to reside in a dwelling unit. Each unit must provide a minimum of 150 square feet of floor space to accommodate its first occupant and a minimum of 100 square feet for every additional occupant. The total habitable room area must form the basis for calculation of floor space.

Every room used for the purpose of sleeping by one occupant in one dwelling unit must have a minimum of 70 square feet of floor space and in case of more than one occupant, must have a minimum of 50 square feet of floor space for every occupant.

Heat

If the landlord provides heating facility, then the tenant is entitled to enjoy heat in the period between September 16 and June 14. Each room has to be heated to a temperature level of at least 68°F during 7.00 am to 11.00 pm and at least 64°F for the rest of the time. The maximum permissible heating level is 78°F during the heating season.

Water

The landlord is required to provide enough water with sufficient pressure to fulfill ordinary needs. The hot water is to be maintained at a temperature level ranging from 110°F to 130°F.

Kitchens

The landlord is required to provide within the kitchen, a sink of appropriate size and capacity for the purpose of washing dishes and utensils; one stove and oven each in good working condition (unless specified otherwise in the written lease) and provision for refrigerator installation. The landlord may not provide a refrigerator but if provided, it must be maintained in working condition.

Cockroaches and Rodents

The landlord is required to ensure that the dwelling unit is free from rodents, cockroaches and such other insect infestation.

Structural Elements

It is the obligation of every landlord to ensure that the structural elements of every unit such as the foundation, doors, windows, ceilings, floors, walls, roof, chimneys, staircases, porches etc. are maintained well to exclude wind, rain and snow; be water-tight, weather-proof, rodent-free, devoid of chronic dampness and in a condition that is fit for habitation in every way.

Snow Removal

Each exit used or intended to be used by occupants of every individual dwelling or rooming unit must be maintained in an obstruction-free condition.

Shutoff Rights

The landlord is not allowed to remove or shutoff any utilities, except on a temporary basis during emergencies or for the purpose of carrying out repairs. If the utility account of a landlord is liable to be shutoff due to non-payment of bills, the utility company is required to inform the tenant 30 days prior to such scheduled termination. The tenant may be required to bear part payment for such overdue bills and then deduct that amount from their rent.

Complete CMR in appendix

FREE OF SANITARY AND BUILDING CODE VIOLATIONS

(M.G.L. c.143, §51 & M.G.L. c. 148A, §2)

A building code states the rules for ensuring minimal safety for buildings and other structures. In Massachusetts, the Board of Building Regulations and Standards (BBRS) formulate regulations and provisions included in the building code. The purpose of this code is to protect the public by ensuring that the construction of buildings is sound and proper, they have adequate routes for exit in case of a fire and offer safety and sanitation overall.

Building codes are followed for a purpose and if not observed they could cause injury to people residing or working in the buildings. Often, tenants, guests or clients are harmed on account of building code violations and are liable to recover full damages according to the theory of premises liability. In Massachusetts, a building code violation is treated as a property owner's negligence if the violation is found to have contributed, in some manner, to causing the injury. For example, if a landlord violated the fire-egress specifications resulting in burn injuries to a person due to his or her inability to escape the burning building, the building code violation is treated as evidence of negligence.

Building code violations may be pertaining to;

> ➢ Sprinkler systems

> ➢ Electrical Wiring

> ➢ Fire Escape

> ➢ Gas Fitting

> ➢ Elevators

> ➢ Exit Signs

> ➢ Emergency Lighting

> ➢ Exterior Locks and

> ➢ Structural Defects etc.

Both Sanitary and Building Code violations are strictly enforced through the 'Implied Warranty of Habitability'. This is a multi-dimensional legal model that integrates the principles of contract and tort along with the State building and sanitary codes. It imposes a legal obligation on the landlord of a residential premise, in terms of an implied agreement, with the aim of ensuring compliance by a rental unit with the State building and sanitary codes during the lease period. If a tenant contracts an injury due to a code violation related to the premises then the landlord is held liable in accordance with the implied warranty of habitability.

A lease agreement cannot include any provision to waive off such an implied warranty.

AVOID WASTE

(Bill H.758, §§ 1-16)

The Massachusetts Department of Environmental Protection (MassDEP) has formulated a commercial organics waste ban that will be effective October 1, 2014.

According to MassDEP estimates, food waste forms about 15 percent of the total municipal solid waste disposed in Massachusetts or approximately 900,000 tons per annum. Including other organic matter such as compostable paper and yard scraps hikes the combined organics to 25 percent of the total disposal. Many businesses have turned to composting to save waste disposal costs. Composting benefits the local community and the entire planet by reducing GHG emitted from landfills.

Avoiding creation of garbage eliminates the worry of disposing or recycling it. Changing a person's habits is at the core of preventing waste. There are several ways in which generating of waste can be reduced while shopping, playing or working. Reducing waste helps save time and money while contributing significantly towards the environment. Some of the ways in which this can be achieved are;

Reducing Household Waste

1. Avoid Disposables

   Opt for re-usable household products instead of disposable ones wherever possible. For example, prefer reusable cups, vessels and napkins etc. Pack your school or office lunch in a reusable container instead of sandwich bags. When buying products, choose items made from recycled material as much as possible and help conserve natural resources.

2. Carry Re-usable Bags

   Carry your own re-usable bags while shopping for groceries and other needs. Many grocers reward their patrons for making use of re-usable bags and help recycle used plastic bags. For small items avoid using a bag.

3. Go Paper-free

   Embrace online billing. Opt for electronic copies of bank statements, newspapers, newsletters and magazines etc. Minimize junk emails.

4. Use Re-usable Bottles

   Carry and consume water, juices and other beverages in re-usable bottles instead of disposable ones.

5. Purchase in Bulk

   Purchase in bulk and pick products that have minimal packaging. Buy boxes or bags of cereal and snacks instead of small single packs.

6. Opt for Concentrates or Powders

   When purchasing juices, lemonade etc., opting for concentrates and powders reduces household waste and lowers grocery bills. These are comparatively inexpensive than cartons.

7. Don't Dispose. Donate for Re-use

Items useless for one person may be useful for another. Consider the possibility of donating items like household goods, children's toys, clothes, sporting goods, appliances, furniture and books etc.

8. Compost Kitchen Leftovers

Composting kitchen leftovers and food scraps significantly reduce household waste and contribute to the environment. For example, kitchen leftovers such as tea bags, fruits, vegetables, coffee grounds, cereals, corn cobs etc. are ideal for composting.

9. Develop Eco-friendly Cleaning Products

Household products such as baking soda, almond oil, lemon juice, corn starch and white vinegar are great alternatives for several cleaning products. Besides lowering the budget these benefit the environment as well.

10. Find Alternative Uses

Items that are no longer needed can be put to alternative uses through creative ideas.

Reducing Packaging Waste

1. Select products that include minimal packaging, least or zero materials.

2. Purchase the biggest size practically required for use and possible storage.

3. Avoid bottled water. Drink tap water, especially where health and safety standards are strictly adhered.

4. Replace liquids with concentrates, wherever possible, such as frozen juice or detergent powder.

5. Carry mugs and avoid bags as far as possible.

SECURITY DEPOSIT - 5% INTEREST - PAID ANNUALLY (M.G.L. c. 186, §15B)

A security deposit given to a landlord as a part of a residential lease continues to be the tenant's property for the entire lease period. Any landlord who accepts a security deposit becomes automatically bound by conclusive legal norms as stated below;

✓ Such security deposit has to be deposited in a Massachusetts bank account bearing interest and should not be mixed with the other assets of the landlord (lessor).

✓ Such security deposit has to be put safely into an account inaccessible by any claims of the landlord's creditors.

✓ For every security deposit, the landlord is not required to hold a separate escrow account.

✓ A detailed record of all security deposits accepted over the previous two years must be maintained by the landlord. Such records must bear the dates, damage descriptions, repairs details and receipts and must be provided for inspection to any tenant or prospective tenant following a reasonable notice.

✓ The landlord must provide the tenant a written receipt within 30 days or accepting a security deposit.

✓ Such a receipt must include the deposit amount; date or receipt by the landlord or landlord's agent; name of the landlord and the landlord's representative accepting the deposit, if other than the landlord; address, unit number and other description of the leased premises; signature of the person accepting the deposit; name, location and account number of the Massachusetts bank where the security deposit amount is deposited.

The landlord's failure to comply with the above stated legal requirements will entitle the tenant to immediately receive back the security deposit.

Further, the landlord is required to provide the tenant a written statement of condition, within 10 days from the start of the lease, describing the current condition of the leased premises, in detail.

The landlord has to pay interest to the tenant at the rate of 5 percent or less, as received by the bank holding the security deposit. Interest has to be paid annually or within 30 days if the lease is terminated before completion of one year.

The landlord has to return the security deposit to the tenant within 30 days after lease termination, but may deduct pending dues from the security deposit such as;

➢ Any unpaid rent or water duties.

➢ Any residual portion of real estate taxes caused due to hike and in accordance with the tenant's obligation to pay as per the lease agreement.

> ➢ Any reasonable repair charges for damage caused to the unit by the tenant, apart from regular wear and tear. In such cases, the landlord is required to provide a detailed itemized account of the repairs including the nature of damage, corrective measures, cost estimates, invoices and receipts etc.

OPTIONS

On reading this section completely, you will understand;

- What is Town Approval?
- What is the Right of First Refusal?

DEFINE –

Options

An 'option contract', also known as 'option', is a promise that fulfills the mandatory criteria for creation of a legal contract and restricts the promisor's authority to revoke an offer made. It is a type of contract that safeguards an offeree from the revocation of a contract by an offeror.

It is a right to convey property. The person granting such an option is termed as 'optionor' (or grantor) and the person benefitting from such an option is termed as 'optionee' (or beneficiary).

For example, in a lease option – also known as a rent-to-buy or rent-to-own option – a landlord-seller leases the property to a tenant-buyer, who has the option to purchase the property at a pre-agreed price, within an agreed time, before the lease ends. When the time expires or the lease ends, the option expires too. The core components of a lease option agreement are the lease term, the buying price, the initial payment and the rent credit.

There are two key components in a lease option;

1. A standard lease agreement that specifies the monthly rental and other common lease terms and
2. The Purchase option that bestows on the Buyer the right to buy the property at a pre-agreed price subject to the Buyer complying with the agreement terms.

EX. TOWN APPROVAL

Executive Town Approval is the process followed for seeking approval of the Town Meeting for the budget recommended by the Board of Selectmen or the Finance Committee. The moderator reads out each budget item, calls out for objections or a vote to pass it. This is done for all the budget items listed. All budget items without any objections and voted in favor, are approved. For those budget items where objections are raised, a debate is encouraged, amendments are made to the budget item and a vote is sought thereafter for approving them.

RIGHT OF FIRST REFUSAL

In case of a 'lease option', also known as a 'right to purchase option', the tenant gets the right to buy the property at a particular price within a specific time period. When the time period ends, the option expires.

Right of First Refusal (ROFR) is a variation of the 'lease option'. This bestows on the tenant the right to buy the property at the same price and on the same terms and conditions as those offered by another party.

In other words, right of first refusal means a restriction on the property owner's right to sell off the property to a prospective third party buyer. The owner is required to offer the same price and terms to the ROFR holder as offered to the third party buyer. The person holding the ROFR may choose to purchase the property or refuse it.

A right of first refusal bears no impact on the land or property usage. There is no covenant running along with the land, hence no binding on future property owners. A ROFR is usually a personal contractual obligation benefitting only certain people who are identified by their name or relationship. It is binding only upon the parties involved in the contract. ROFR carries a time limitation which, upon expiry, renders it ineffective and uncovers the restrictions on the sale or disposition of the property by the owner unless there are other clauses affecting such a sale.

ROFR is commonly found in cases of divorce where the judge includes it in the divorce settlement if the home is jointly owned or the partners agree to a ROFR when selling the home. In certain situations, where a family home is put up for sale, parents set up an ROFR for their children. While drafting a ROFR or purchasing a property subject to a ROFR, it must be checked thoroughly by a legal professional to ensure language clarity; concise and precise mention of the right; correct statement of the factors triggering it or rendering it ineffective.

There is some uncertainty however about the entitlement of the ROFR holder to assert it after having declined it the first time. For example, if the holder declined the ROFR on a sale offer that fails eventually due to any reason such as a bad inspection or the prospective buyer backing out, does the ROFR hold good for future offers? Most attorneys may advise the property owner to continue the ROFR for future offers even in case of prior refusals.

PROPERTY MANAGEMENT

On reading this section completely, you will understand;

- What is Specialty property?
- What is Management Division?
- The key responsibilities of property management.

DEFINE, SPECIALTY, MANAGEMENT DIVISION

Property Management (M.G.L. c. 183A, §10)

Property Management is the operation and maintenance of residential, commercial or industrial real estate. It also involves management of personal property, tools, equipment and physical capital assets procured and used to build, repair and maintain property. It comprises systems, processes and manpower necessary for managing the lifecycle of all property including acquisition, control, maintenance, responsibility, accountability, utilization and disposition. In simple words, it is the management of the common areas of a building or condominium, done as directed by the Board of Trustees or Board of Directors.

Property Management also means activities undertaken by a third party for a property owner, as per an agreement and in return for a fee, commission, compensation or such other valuable consideration, for marketing, leasing, physical administration, financial handling and overall maintenance of real estate or supervision thereof.

Specialty

Property management involves different specialties such as management of residential property, commercial property or industrial property, individual buildings or a group of buildings (complexes) etc. A building manager is a person who manages operation and maintenance of commercial building(s) belonging to firms or institutions or condominiums where unit owners operate businesses and not used for residential purposes. In contrast, a residential manager is a person who manages the daily operation and maintenance of a residential building, be it a condominium with residential units or an individual owners home. Besides this basic difference between the two, there are some differences (and similarities) in the role and responsibilities, education and skills required and work experience desired for these to property management positions. These are listed below;

Building Manager

The building manager is primarily responsible for tactical decision and operations management of the building facilities of commercial businesses or institutions and their construction activities. The building manager is the single point of contact for all daily activities concerning the facilities. The key objective of the building manager is to ensure a high quality of service delivery consistently aligned with the business needs.

Key responsibilities include;

- ✓ Manage on-site maintenance staff, vendors and external service providers, different committees, inclement weather experts, building announcements, capital and operating budgets and action plans.
- ✓ Ensure service delivery by the service providers that is in line with expected service levels and necessary standards, within the agreed costs.
- ✓ Liaise with various business units to ensure consistent delivery and timely as well as accurate fulfillment of occupants' needs.
- ✓ Proactively develop and enhance service delivery standards to retain the leading edge.
- ✓ Ensure adequate support to all business units through reliable delivery.
- ✓ Work in collaboration with business units to ensure development and implementation of building and ground maintenance plans to fulfill their needs.
- ✓ Implement assessment programs to offer quick and efficient review of building-related concerns, thus minimizing decision-making time.
- ✓ Supervise service providers and ongoing maintenance activities to ensure agreed contract.
- ✓ Manage energy consumption to consistently achieve high standards and benchmark them regularly with established norms and milestones.
- ✓ Develop facilities management processes to ensure conformance to desired service levels in sync with the prevailing conditions, equipment, structure and plant etc.
- ✓ Devise and implement a detailed and accurate reporting mechanism to ensure delivery of key information to various business units.
- ✓ Manage the facilities module of the implemented technology platform with core purpose of capturing and presenting portfolio lifecycle information.

Education & Experience

- ✓ Preferably a Bachelor's degree in engineering or in a business discipline.
- ✓ At least 10 years of work experience in a similar role in building management with hands-on experience of managing large properties and maintenance program management.

Knowledge & Skills

- ✓ In-depth knowledge of buildings and systems and complexity of operations.

- ✓ Deep understanding of building construction, repairs and maintenance.
- ✓ Business and financial acumen combined with a sound track record of managing large properties or contracts.
- ✓ A good grasp of environmental considerations concerning to the created environment, legislative and other requirements etc.
- ✓ Ability to devise, implement and manage facilities management activities and programs.
- ✓ Ability to work as part of a team for delivering quality consistently.
- ✓ A good understanding of business processes and requirements for an effective support mechanism.
- ✓ Strong negotiating skills.
- ✓ Good people management and interpersonal skills.

Residential Manager

The residential manager is responsible for the day-to-day operations of the residential properties under his or her charge.

Some of the key responsibilities are;

- ✓ Supervise the daily activities of the sales / marketing, maintenance, leasing and other support staff.
- ✓ Provide information regarding operating costs and annual budget for the properties managed.
- ✓ Possibly develop and implement programs to increase occupancy and renewal rates for leases.
- ✓ Good knowledge of a wide range of concepts, procedures and practices related to property management.
- ✓ Extensive experience and sound judgment to set and achieve goals.
- ✓ Perform a range of tasks associated with property management.
- ✓ Lead and direct other staff working in allied areas or activities.
- ✓ Possess and exhibit good creativity and latitude in daily operations.
- ✓ Report effectively to the owner or board members.

Education & Experience

- ✓ Preferably have a Bachelor's Degree and work experience of at least 5 years in a similar field.

Management Division

Property Management Agreement

A property management contract should be drafted in clear, unambiguous language and must;

> List all relevant terms and conditions of the services, duties, responsibilities and obligations of the property management firm towards the real estate owner.
> Be duly signed by either the property owner or their agent and the broker designated by the property management firm or that broker's authorized property licensee.
> Include a starting and ending date for the contract / transaction.
> Comprise provision for cancellation that are mutually agreed by both the parties.
> Specify the method of disposition of all the fees and charges collected by the property management company, including tenant deposits.
> Mention the type and frequency of submission of status reports to the property owner.
> State the amount and purpose of all financial elements that the property management company possesses
> Make provision for the disbursal and allocation of the interest earned on the money accumulated in the trust account.
> Specify the terms and conditions of the compensation that the real estate owner will be required to pay for the services rendered in accordance with the property management agreement.
> Not be assigned to a different licensee or licensed party without the express written consent from the property owner.
> Ideally include a provision for automatic renewal, if the property owner is sent a reminder notice by the property management firm at least 30 days prior to the renewal date. Such a notice will not negate any other cancellation conditions agreed upon otherwise.
> Provision for a reasonable amount of liquidated damages or cancellation charges in case of early termination of the contract.
> Empower the broker of the property management firm to authorize a licensed or unlicensed individual, in their direct employment, to be signatory on or transfer money to the property management trust account in which the firm deposits the property owner's money.
> Usually mandate two or more signatures on the checks issued from the property management account.
> Encompass all other provisions agreed upon between the property owner and the property management firm that are not conflicting or contradictory in nature.

Management Fees Calculation

Although there is a substantial difference between the property management fees of commercial and residential property, the average management fee ranges from 4% to 12 % of the monthly rent. In case of single family home, the owner may pay up to 10% of the rent derived from the property as management fees. The amount of fees usually varies depending on the number of properties being managed, number of individual units in each property, the location and overall condition of the property and the services rendered. Property management fees may also differ across cities and states.

The fee structure can be of different types such as flat fees, hybrid fees (combination of flat fee and percentage) requiring payment of lesser / greater of the two.

COLLECT RENTS, PAY BILLS, PREPARE REPORTS

The property manager or the property management company works in close conjunction with the Board members to enforce the Association's policies, rules and regulations; identify issues requiring attention and resolving them. They also work towards defining goals, drawing plans and strategies to achieve them, organize and lead projects for implementation and track results. Some of the key responsibilities executed on a regular basis include;

Collect Rents

The property manager or the management company collects and deposits rents and association / condominium fees as per schedule, sends monthly statements to defaulting owners and invokes legal options in cases of acute payment defaults. All the collected amounts are deposited into an exclusive bank account.

Pay Bills

It is the responsibility of the property manager or the property management company to pay the bills related to common area utilities and even individual units wherever applicable. Bills pertaining to water charges, property taxes, gas, electricity, heat etc. are paid as per the responsibilities stated in the agreements.

Prepare Reports

The property management company or the property manager is responsible for maintaining records of all receipts and disbursements; accounting of individual units; fulfill legal requirements pertaining to Chapter 400 (Super Lien Law) to satisfy foreclosure protection; prepare 6d certificates, FNMA questionnaires and a correspondence file.

Report preparation duties also include financial reports such as unit holder account balances, collection status, balance sheets, bank reconciliation, accounts payable, collection status, reserve reports and income statement (actual vs budgeted) etc.

Miscellaneous

On reading this section completely, you will understand;

- What is the difference between property assignment and subletting?
- The status of leases when leased property has to be sold.
- What is a 99 year lease?

Assign vs Sublet

In the case of a lease agreement, some unforeseen issues may compel the tenant to move out of the leased premises prior to the end of the agreed term and avoid paying rent for the balance term or to give up part of the rental premises while still occupying the rest. Since it is not possible to anticipate such circumstances, the best thing to do is to ensure maximum flexibility in the lease agreement. This can be achieved by including an assignment and sublet clause in the lease agreement which provides a mechanism to the tenant, without breaching the terms of the lease, to assign full or part of his or her leasehold estate or sublet it prior to end of the lease term.

Both, assigning and subletting involve transferring the lease obligations to a new tenant, however, they differ in certain legal and practical aspects. A majority of leases prohibit assigning and subleasing without the owners consent

Assign

In the event of an assignment, the tenant transfers the entire set of leasehold rights to a new tenant (assignee) for the remaining part of the lease term. Unless restricted by the lease, tenant may assign to any person and charge any rent as desired. The assignee then has to remit the rent to the landlord directly. But the original tenant still bears the liability for payment of the rent if the assignee fails to pay, unless the landlord absolves him or her from the original liability.

Sublet

In the event of a sublet or sublease, usually only a part of the leased premises are sub-let while the original tenant continues to occupy the rest of the premises. However, the entire rental may also be transferred for the balance term of the lease, while the original tenant moves out. As in an assignment, the tenant may choose to sub-let to any person and charge any rent. The person who subleases is called a 'sub-tenant'. The sub-tenant has to pay rent to the sub-lessor, who in turn has to pay rent to the landlord. If the sub-tenant fails to pay the rent, the tenant (sub-lessor) has the right to terminate the sub-lease, evict the sub-tenant and reclaim the space. And if the sub-tenant violates any clause of the original tenant lease agreement, then the landlord has the right to terminate it.

Most leases disallow assignments or subletting, but if they permit, they usually require the landlord's approval. However, if the lease agreement does not specify any terms and conditions about assignments or subletting, then they are permitted.

The original lessee's interest is called a *sandwich lease*.

SALE OF PROPERTY RE STATUS OF LEASES

Landlords and property managers always like rent-paying, harmless tenants. But sometimes circumstances may compel the landlord to sell the house or building with the tenant. Having a tenant limits the landlord's market to primarily investors because the tenant has to be sold along with the house. Any party buying the rental property automatically becomes a landlord until the tenant's lease expires, whether they like it or not.

What options does the landlord have for selling off a rental property occupied by a tenant?

1) Sell the real estate after the tenant's lease expires

Waiting until the tenant's lease expires is the best option if the landlord can afford it. This is a costly option since no rent is received during the time leading up to the sale; however this option offers the greatest possibility of a quick sale at a higher price. The property can be sold to both investors and homeowners, so there is no limitation. Being unoccupied, the property can be fixed-up or refreshed to give it the best appearance and make it show-ready. Besides, there will not be a tell-all tenant telling prospective buyers things that they should not know about the property.

2) Sell the real estate along with the tenant

This is the cheapest but the most difficult option. The landlord will require the cooperation of the tenant for the sale of the property as the tenant will be still occupying it. The property cannot be sold to a prospective buyer wanting to move in immediately, since the tenant's lease has to be honored. The landlord has to either sell it to someone who is either willing to wait for the tenant's lease to expire or an investor looking for regular income from the property. The landlord is advised to not upgrade anything although he or she can obtain a higher price by applying fresh paint, installing a new roof and carpet. Upgrading the kitchen, bathroom, appliances or other expensive items is not advised since that would incur more costs and investors are usually not willing to pay additional costs when buying rental property.

3) Sell the real estate to the tenant

This option is like setting on a journey without knowing the destination. Most of the tenants prefer to rent because they usually cannot afford to buy a property or just don't wish to. If the landlord is not in a hurry to cash-in from the sale of the property then the option of owner-financing is open. But if the tenant is unable to find a bank willing to finance the purchase of the property, there is a probable risk. The landlord has to be prepared to take back the property in case of a default in payment of installments. This option is not viable, especially as a second mortgage, considering the currently prevailing default rate.

NINETY-NINE YEAR LEASE

A lease for 100 years or greater is deemed to be freehold or fee-simple estate. Hence the longest lease term is restricted to 99 years.

A 99-year lease is just a long-term lease and its benefit depends on the terms of the specific lease. Lease terms may vary on the basis of it being a residential or commercial lease. In this type of a lease the term of years simply conveys the idea that the lease will be effective during the life of the tenant since the lifespan of most people does not exceed 99 years.

A long-term lease, which is theoretically indefinite, provides an individual the security of property ownership without actually having to buy the property. The reasons for long-term leasing instead of purchasing real property could be many, but the most prominent reason among these is to prevent an outright sale since it may be forbidden. For example, some countries may permit only its citizens to own land, hence non-citizens wishing to reside long-term or permanently will have to enter into long-term leases. Another benefit is that the lease payment may be locked-in at a low level as compared to a short-term lease or mortgage payment which may fluctuate with the interest rates and the property market. At times, such long-term leases are used for gifting properties or as mechanisms for planning tax or real estate issues.

Although the 99-year lease appears to be linked to individual lifespan, it is not restricted to individual use only. Such long-term leases are commonly found in the commercial space, for businesses, instead of individual residential purpose. Private firms often resort to long-term leases in order to make use of federal land. For example, location-sensitive businesses such as bars and restaurants may enter into long-term leases since their business success depends on the location that they operate from.

SPECIAL ATTENTION TO LEAD PAINT, SMOKE DETECTORS, DISCRIMINATION
*to be Covered in Detail in Future Modules

On reading this section completely, you will understand;

- Everything about the Lead Paint Law.
- Laws related to Smoke Detectors.
- Laws pertaining to Discrimination.

LEAD PAINT

Several incidents of young children being poisoned by lead paint are recorded every year in Massachusetts. Lead poisoning can permanently damage the brain, nervous system and kidneys of a child. It can also lead to severe learning disabilities and behavioral disorders. The Lead Law safeguards the right of a child to dwell in a lead-safe home.

The Lead Law mandates the removal or covering of hazards that lead paint can possibly cause, in homes constructed prior to 1978, where children below the age of six reside. Examples of lead paint hazards include lead paint lying loose, lead paint applied on windows or other surfaces that is within the reach of children. Owners are responsible for lead law compliance, including owners of rental property and those residing in single family homes. Financial assistance is available in the form of tax credits, loans and grants.

The property owner can ensure compliance with the Lead Law in two ways, as explained below;

1. Remove or cover all lead related hazards. For this, the owner has to first hire the services of a licensed lead inspector for testing the home for lead and listing all the lead hazards present. On approval of the work the property owner is issued a Letter of Full Compliance.

2. Get the potentially harmful lead hazards rectified, while keeping the remaining hazards under control. This is known as 'interim control'. The owner has to first hire the service of a licensed risk assessor to determine the type and amount of work required for interim control. On approval of the work, the property owner is issued a Letter of Interim Control. Following this, the property owner is given a time of two years to remove or cover the remaining lead hazards and obtain a Letter of Full Compliance.

The work of removing or covering of lead hazards has to be executed by a licensed deleader, although an owner or agent (without deleader's license) is allowed to perform certain tasks. However, the property owner or agent cannot execute any tasks until;

1. A licensed lead inspector completes inspection of the home.

2. They acquire appropriate training for executing the deleading work.

The rental property owner is legally responsible if a child gets poisoned by lead hazards at his home. The owner cannot escape liability by getting the tenants to sign an agreement indicating acceptance of the lead paint. The owner's best protection from liability is compliance with the Lead Law,

SMOKE DETECTORS (M.G.L. c. 148, §§ 26F, 28F)

Massachusetts laws specify minimum standards for different automated fire, heat and smoke detection systems in every residential and commercial property. Most of the home fires are found to occur at night, besides the smell of smoke is observed to numb the senses, inducing deeper sleep.

Massachusetts General Law (M.G.L. c. 148, § 26F) decrees that following the sale or transfer of particular homes, the seller is required to install smoke detectors of approved types. Such requirements are applicable to homes built or modified before the Massachusetts State Building Code (January 1, 1975) came into effect. If a building has been subjected to any additions, modifications or renovation after January 1, 1975, the date mentioned on the building permit defines the smoke detector requirements pertaining to the building code. The transfer law is applicable to buildings comprising five or less housing units.

A sale of any residential building comprising five or less dwelling units cannot be executed without inspection of the installed smoke detectors. All such inspections are administered by the chief of the local fire department. On satisfactory inspection the chief of the fire department issues a Certificate of Compliance. The original certificate document is required at the time of closing of the sale. It is the seller's obligation to bear the costs incurred and obtain the certificate, unless stated otherwise in the sale agreement. The state building code determines the installation requirements of the smoke detectors depending on the date of construction of the residential unit. Some homes may need battery-powered smoke detectors, while others may require only interconnected hard-wired detectors or both combined. Yet other homes may need interconnected hard-wired smoke detectors having battery-power backup. Residential units constructed after 1998 are required to include battery-power backup. Massachusetts State Law establishes the maximum fee for conducting inspection of smoke detectors.

From April 5, 2010, the Massachusetts smoke detector requirements witnessed a significant change, applicable to all residential units within the ambit of M.G.L. c. 148, § 28F on being sold or transferred. All smoke detectors installed within a distance of 20 feet from a kitchen or bathroom (consisting of a bathtub or shower) has to be of the photoelectric type only. This will mitigate the risk of generating false alarms due to steam and cooking. All smoke detectors installed beyond 20 feet from a kitchen or bathroom (consisting of a bathtub or shower) must be of either of the following types;

> A Dual detector (that uses both, ionization as well as photoelectric technologies)

   OR

> Two separate detectors (One of Photoelectric type and the other of Ionization type)

In housing units constructed after January 1975, hence not subjected to M.G.L. c. 148, § 26F, upgrading the smoke detectors is recommended but not mandated by law.

DISCRIMINATION (M.G.L. c. 151B)

If the Massachusetts Commission Against Discrimination (MCAD) finds out that a licensee has resorted to unlawful means or committed an unlawful act in violation of the Massachusetts Fair Housing law during his or her tenure as a licensee, then it issues a notice to the Board. On receiving such a notice, the board will suspend the guilty licensee for duration of 60 days. If this violation by the licensee has occurred within a period of two years from the date of a similar prior violation of the Massachusetts Fair Housing law, then MCAD will notify the Board and the Board will suspend the broker's or salesperson's license for a duration of 90 days.

The Massachusetts Commission Against Discrimination (MCAD) is a law enforcement agency for civil rights. It is empowered to investigate and judge cases of discrimination in the areas of employment, credit, services, housing, public accommodations and education. Further, MCAD propagates rules and regulations, tracks and aids businesses and governments in ensuring compliance of civil rights laws, promotes knowledge of human rights and sponsors educational and training programs for law enforcement personnel responsible for enforcement of civil rights. MCAD comprises of three members selected by the governor for a term of three years.

Any individual lodging a complaint pertaining to a violation of Massachusetts anti-discriminatory laws allegedly by an employee, is required to do so in less than 300 days from such discriminatory act. If a complaint pertains to housing discrimination, it has to be lodged within 12 months of the occurrence. If the MCAD confirms that a person has indulged in an unlawful act, it may impose a civil penalty on that person along with any other sanctions, for an amount not exceeding;

> $10,000, if it is a first offense.

> $25,000, if it is a second offense, committed within duration of five years.

> $50,000, if it is a third offense, committed within duration of seven years.

Housing discrimination in the following categories is illegal under Massachusetts Law;

Section 8 or Public Assistance

It is illegal to deny renting to a person simply due to him or her being a recipient under Section 8; or public assistance from federal, state or local bodies (e.g. SSI, Food Stamps, TAFDC, Welfare etc.); or medical assistance; or any other local, state or federal housing subsidy (e.g. MRVP, Chapter 707 etc.).

This law also restricts discrimination on account of any requirements involved in taking public or rental assistance and housing grant programs. For example, a property owner is not allowed to deny signing of a lease or inspection of an apartment if a state or federal rental program mandates such requirements. Refusing acceptance of housing vouchers provided by specific housing authorities, by a landlord, is also deemed illegal. This law is applicable to all types of properties, including owner-occupied duplexes.

Sexual Orientation

Discriminating against someone on the basis of his or her sexual orientation is considered illegal. Massachusetts Fair Housing laws categorize Sexual Orientation as a protected class. It is also a special focus area for the Department of Housing and Urban Development (HUD), which is now actively involved, for the first time, in a historic research activity to investigate housing discrimination on the basis of sexual orientation and gender identity.

Gender Identity and Expression

Similar to Sexual Orientation, Gender Identity and Expression is also a protected class according to the Massachusetts Fair Housing laws. This too is a focus area, for the first time, for the Department of Housing and Urban Development (HUD).

Marital Status

Discriminating against a person on the basis of his or her marital status is termed illegal. Marital Status too falls in the protected category within the Massachusetts Fair Housing laws.

Military or Veteran Status

Discrimination against an individual due to him or her being a veteran or a part of the armed forces is deemed illegal.

Age

Discriminating against anyone on the basis of his or her age is illegal. Age is classified in the protected category under the Massachusetts Fair Housing laws, with a few exceptions. Protection is not extended to minors or residents of state and federally-aided housing facilities for the elderly or housing facilities for persons aged 55 years or over or individuals aged 62 years or over.

Ancestry

Discriminating against a person on account of his or her ancestry is considered illegal. Ancestry is categorized as a protected class under the Massachusetts Fair Housing law.

CHAPTER 3

KEY TERMS

Contracts	Consideration	Competency
Revocation	Purchase & Sale	Statute of Frauds
Breach of Contract	Specific Performance	Quitclaim
Granting Clause	Legal Description	Metes & Bounds
Proper Execution	Damages	Equitable Title

CHAPTER 3 LEARNING OBJECTIVES

1. What is a Chain of Title?
2. What is an Abstract of Title?
3. What are Massachusetts tax stamps?
4. What are the applicable tax rates on deed transfers?
5. What is a Torrens System of property registration?
6. What is the significance of a Land Court?
7. What is the meaning of Certificate of Title and why is it required?
8. What is a low book and page reference?
9. What is the granting clause with respect to a deed?
10. What the meaning of 'Consideration' in a property deed?
11. How is the transfer of rights explained in a deed?
12. What is legal description of property and how is it described in a deed?
13. What are the requirements for proper execution of a deed?
14. Who is a grantor and grantee in a property deed?
15. What is the county registry of deeds?
16. What is a book and page reference?
17. What is specific performance in relation to a breach of contract?
18. Why and when is a deposit retained if a contract is breached?
19. What is the Right to Assign?
20. What do price / consideration mean in a property transaction?
21. What, when and how much about deposits related to property deals?
22. The importance of dates in a property transaction.
23. In what kind of situations is a deed considered void?
24. Under what conditions does a deed become voidable?
25. What happens to an offer when its time limit expires?
26. What happens when an Offeror withdraws an offer?
27. Why does an Offer terminate on Acceptance by the grantee?
28. Why does an Offer terminate on revocation by the Offeree?
29. What happens in case of a Counteroffer?
30. What is Offer and Acceptance with respect to a Contract?
31. What does a Consideration in a Contract mean?
32. What is the meaning of Competency?
33. What is a Listing?
34. What constitutes a Purchase & Sale Agreement?

35. What is the meaning of Lease and Deed?
36. What is a Mortgage Note / Deed?

CONTRACTS/DEEDS

On reading this section completely, you will understand;

- What is a Listing?
- What constitutes a Purchase & Sale Agreement?
- What is the meaning of Lease and Deed?
- What is a Mortgage Note?
- What is a Mortgage Deed?
- What are Options?

LISTING, PURCHASE AND SALE, LEASE, DEED

TYPES OF LISTING AGREEMENTS

The listing agreement is an employment contract between the property seller and the real estate broker. It includes the essential elements of the contract such as;

- ✓ It establishes the relationship between the principal and the agent and specifies their rights and responsibilities.

- ✓ It fixes the property price and the commission rate that he broker will be paid.

- ✓ It specifies whether the seller permits or restricts the broker from liaising with the buyer's broker.

- ✓ Whether a multiple listing service (MLS) will be allowed to be used and

- ✓ Whether a lock box will be can be placed on the property.

6 types of listing agreements are:

Open Listing

An open listing is almost like a "for sale by owner" listing. The seller offers to pay a sales commission only to the first one *(procuring cause)* who brings an acceptable purchase agreement. No commission is owed to any agent if the seller finds a buyer on his own. This listing provides the least amount of protection for an agent because the agent is in competition with the seller to market the property. The seller can withdraw the listing without notice.

There are two types of exclusive agreements. To be enforced, an exclusive agreement must be in writing and contain a termination date.

Exclusive Agency Listing

In an exclusive agency listing, the seller contracts with one agent to sell the home. If that agent, or any other licensed cooperating agent finds an acceptable buyer, the seller must pay a sales commission. Similarly to an open listing, if the home seller finds a buyer on his own, no commission is due an agent. *Exclusive to everyone except the seller.*

Exclusive Right-to-Sell Listing

A majority of real estate listings are this type. The listing agent has 100 percent control of the transaction. In all cases of a sale (the seller, the listing agent or a cooperating selling agent finds an acceptable buyer), the listing agent will earn the commission. If another cooperating agent is involved, the commission is typically split between the agents. *Exclusive to everyone, including the seller.*

Co-broker Listing (Multiple Listing)

A marketing tool for all agents is the multiple listing service (MLS). The MLS distributes listing information and photos via the computer to members who are working with appropriate buyers. In Massachusetts, MLS listings are also available on the Internet at sites such as www.mlspin.com. Prospective home buyers may research what's for sale on their own by visiting sites such as www.realtor.com. *Note: In Massachusetts, seller must be informed of vicarious liability (liable for the actions of others) if a listing is co-listed with another brokerage.*

Net Listing

A net listing allows the agent to earn a commission that is based on the difference between the final sale price and what the seller agrees to get. A net listing is illegal in some states. Under this agreement, the seller tells their agent the net price they want to walk away with. The agent can then market the property by adding an additional amount that the agent wants to earn or the agent may get an offer well above the net that the seller wanted. **Example:** Agent Caroline agrees to sell Norman's house on a *net listing.* They set the net price at $200,000. Caroline finds a buyer willing and able to pay $310,000. Caroline's commission is $10,000. Note that if Caroline had found a buyer offering $300,000 *(all offers must be presented to the seller)*, Caroline would earn no commission at all.

Net Listings are legal in New York, Pennsylvania, Florida, California

Under the Massachusetts Real Estate License Law, a "Net Listing" is prohibited.

Pocket Listing

Typically referred to as a private listing or off-market listing because it is not listed in the multiple listing service (MLS). The seller and agent have control over who knows about the listing and under what conditions the home may be seen. There can be a detailed written agreement to insure the conditions upon which the property may be presented. Prospective buyers are often asked to sign a confidentiality agreement. *Note: Agents and brokers are not required to belong to an MLS service. They may advertise in other ways and not be considered pocket listings.*

TERMINATING A LISTING

Listing agreements may be cancelled for a variety of reasons (economic, personality clashes, timing), these are the most common:

Expiration of Listing

A valid listing agreement has a beginning date and an end date. When the end date is reached without a successful offer, the seller is not obligated to resign with the same broker. All obligations have been fulfilled under the contract.

Mutual Agreement

If seller and brokerage come to a mutual agreement to cancel the listing, all parties must sign a cancellation agreement. At this point, the property will be removed from MLS and all external advertising will cease. *Note: There may be a period of time, 60-90 days, in which the brokerage will be entitled to payment if a customer they presented (procuring cause) ultimately buys the property. This can be incorporated into the cancellation agreement.*

Abandonment/Performance of Agent

A seller may cancel for breach of contract if the agent or broker does not meet general service requirements under the listing agreement such as: showing the home, being responsive, executing the approved marketing plan or keeping fiduciary responsibility to the seller. The seller's recourse is to make contact with the broker in an effort to resolve the situation. *Note: Incorporating nominal early termination fees ($295 - $595) may be a way to avert going to court.*

Death or insanity

The death of insanity of either party before the end of the contract term may be cancelled without obligation. Death of the agent does not necessarily cancel a contract because the agreement is with the brokerage. If the brokerage goes out of business, the contract may be considered cancelled. If the listing agreement is signed by more than one party and only one party dies, the contract may still be considered valid. If the property goes into escrow and the seller dies, the estate of the seller will be responsible for completing the contract.

Transfer of Title

If the seller's property is transferred due to bankruptcy or foreclosure sale, the listing agreement is effectively cancelled. Divorce agreements may impact the brokerage commissions. *Note: Seller may be liable for commissions if the property is simply transferred to a family member and sold within the contract period. Conditions should be clearly spelled out in the listing agreement.*

Revocation

Both seller and broker may cancel a listing agreement for sufficient cause. If a seller falsely represents his property and/or his interest in it, this presents a valid cause to revoke the contract. If the brokerage agrees to certain conditions via contract and fails to implement them, this is a reason to cancel. Both sides must agree to cancel and both should approve the revocation in writing if a discussion does not remedy the problem. *Note: The agreement should be authorized by the managing broker and not the agent. The seller may be liable for damages (time and expenses)*

War

General provisions in contracts provides that No Party will be liable for failure to perform or delay in performing any obligation (other than the payment of money) under an Agreement if such failure or delay is due to earthquake, terrorist attack, government actions, or war (declared or undeclared). Note: While there isn't a typical war clause in contracts, it is something to speak about with a client.

Destruction of the property

A property that is severely damaged by flood or fire may be taken off the market by mutual agreement.

PURCHASE AND SALE AGREEMENT (M.G.L. c. 184)

The Purchase and Sale (P&S) Agreement is the contract that governs a transaction between a Buyer and a Seller with respect to the property that is being sold / bought. In most cases, the Buyer submits an Offer to the Seller initially, which specifies the contract terms. This is the Offer to Purchase, which specifies the parties' responsibilities during the interim period before the property is delisted from the market and the closing. The Seller accepts the initial Offer to Purchase. However, this is not the final contract. The P&S is signed after the execution of the initial Offer to Purchase. The P&S is more detailed and contains all the terms and conditions that are mutually agreed between the Buyer and the Seller. It is the final contract agreement that is binding on both parties.

In Massachusetts, the Greater Boston Real Estate Board (GBREB) has created a "standard form" purchase and sale agreement, which forms the basis of majority of the real estate transactions. The P&S is a legal document that supersedes the initial offer and is considered as a "long form" contract.

The "standard form" P&S agreement is, in fact, very non-standard, especially from the Buyer's perspective, as it is significantly tilted in favor of the Seller. Hence the attorneys of both parties, especially the Buyer, modify it suitably to create a fair and level playing field.

LEASE (M.G.L. c. 186 §§ 15C-17)

The Massachusetts lease agreement is a contract that extends over a term of one (1) year (customizable, if required) and is binding on the landlord and the tenant in such a way that both have to abide by the terms stated within it. Generally, as long as the rental fee is paid by the tenant each month, he or she is not deemed to be violating any terms of the contract.

After the lease agreement is authorized by both the parties and the security deposit as well as the rent for the first month is paid, the tenant is given possession of the keys and complete access to the premises.

DEED (M.G.L. c. 183A)

A Deed is a legal document that conveys an interest of ownership of a property to a buyer (grantee). It includes details about the Seller (grantor), the Buyer (grantee), the method of taking title (tenancy) by the grantee, the consideration (amount of the purchase price), the property's legal description and a citation to the registry records of the previous deed. The deed is usually drafted by the attorney of the Seller.

DEED COVENANTS
Covenants are promises contained in the deed.

Covenant of Seizin
Grantor guarantees that he is the owner and has the right to sell it.

Covenant of Warranty of Title
Grantor promises to pay for defending the title against rightful claims.

Covenant of Further Assurance
Grantor warrants she will correct deficiencies to perfect the title. i.e. executing new deed to correct a type.

Covenant against Encumbrances
The grantor warrants that there are no defects or claims against the title.

Covenant of Quiet Enjoyment

The grantor warrants the title is free of acts or claims from third parties.

TYPES OF DEEDS

General Warranty Deed

The general warranty deed provides the greatest protection against defects in the title. It includes all deed covenants and provides protections against the title that may have applied before the grantor actually owned the property.

Limited/Special Warranty Deed

Applies a warranty to include only claims that apply during the time the grantor owned the property. Claims arising from periods prior to grantor ownership would not be a liability. For example: The grantor would not be responsible for a lien that was recorded prior to the grantor accepting title.

Quitclaim Deed

This deed contains no expressed or implied warranties of possession or title. It is generally used to clear minor defects or clouds on the title. This deed provides the least amount of protection to the grantee.

Massachusetts Statutory Quitclaim Deed

Quitclaim Covenants in a deed is that same as having limited warranty covenant. *This is referred to as Grant Deed in other regions of the United States.*

Bargain & Sale Deed

Commonly used by fiduciaries, trustees, executors and court officials, while this deed does convey all of the grantor's interest in the property, it contains no expressed or implied warranty to title. The grantor does not warrant that they have possession of or a claim of interest in the property.

Special Purpose Deeds

Sheriff's Deed
Given by a court to satisfy a judgment.

Timber Deed
Used to convey interest in growing timber. Once cut, it becomes personal property.

Fiduciary Deed
Used to execute a court ordered conveyance.

Crops & Perennials
Perennials (shrubs) require a deed to transfer title. Annual crops are emblements and require a bill of sale.

Mortgage Note (M.G.L. c. 183)

A mortgage note is a promise to repay a debt, which is secured by a mortgage, contract or trust deed. When appropriately drafted, such a note can be sold to generate immediate cash. It is common practice to accept a trust deed or mortgage in the form of a note as a part of a property sale proceeds.

Mortgage Deed (M.G.L. c. 183. § 18)

The mortgage deed is a legal document that offers security interest in a real estate to a mortgage lender. A borrower pledges his or her property as security to obtain a loan and the deed denotes the ownership rights of the lender in the pledged real estate. This deed bestows on the lender foreclosure rights to the property in the event that the borrower fails to fulfill the mortgage obligations. All mortgage lenders make borrowers sign a mortgage deed or trust deed at the time of signing of the promissory note and before actual disbursal of loan funds. In Massachusetts, the mortgage lenders must use this document as a means for securing the home loans given out to the borrowers.

Option (M.G.L. c. 184A. § 5)

(Repeated from Module II)

An 'option contract', also known as 'option', is a promise that fulfills the mandatory criteria for creation of a legal contract and restricts the promisor's authority to revoke an offer made. It is a type of contract that safeguards an offeree from the revocation of a contract by an offeror.

It is a right to convey property. The person granting such an option is termed as 'optionor' (or grantor) and the person benefitting from such an option is termed as 'optionee' (or beneficiary).

ESSENTIAL ELEMENTS OF ANY CONTRACT

On reading this section completely, you will understand;

- What is Offer and Acceptance with respect to a Contract?
- What does a Consideration in a Contract mean?
- What are the legalities of a Contract?
- What is the meaning of Competency?
- What is Consent (Duress Notary)?

OFFER AND ACCEPTANCE *(M.G.L. C. 106. § 2-206)*

Offer and Acceptance are vital elements for the drafting of a legally binding contract.

An offer is an expression of willingness, through words or conduct, to enter into a legally binding contract on certain terms and conditions specified in the proposal document, which shall be binding on all the parties involved upon signing it. The person extending such an offer to contract is the 'offeror' and the person to whom the offer is addressed is the "offeree".

An acceptance means agreeing to all the terms and conditions specified in the offer, which culminates in signing of the offer by both parties (offeror and offeree). A legally binding contract is established when the offeree accepts the initial offer made by the offeror or the terms of the initial offer are suitably modified and mutually agreed by both the parties.

An offer to purchase a parcel of land by a person to a land owner and he or she agreeing to the terms and conditions specified in the offer is an example of offer and acceptance.

CONSIDERATION *(M.G.L. C. 106. § 3-303)*

With respect to contracts, 'consideration' is the price or anything of value that is given by the buyer (promisor) of the property to the seller (promisee), as mutually agreed, in a real estate transaction. In other words, each party must give and receive something of value. It could be money, services, physical object, promised activity or abstinence from a specific decision or such other element of value. It is a concept of value usually associated with contracts.

LEGALITY *(M.G.L. C. 255B. § 18)*

Often, property sellers as well as their brokers are under the wrong impression that the offer-to-purchase is a simple formality and that the contract becomes binding on the parties involved only when they sign the more detailed purchase and sale agreement. This is a misconception.

Under Massachusetts Case Law, a 'standard form' offer-to-purchase that is signed by the parties concerned becomes a binding and enforceable contract for sale of real estate even though the initial offer is expected to be followed by a more detailed purchase and sale agreement.

For example, if a seller accepts an offer by signing it and then receives a better deal from another buyer, any disregard towards the original deal is considered illegal. In such a scenario, the buyer can sue the seller for specific performance and record a notice of claim (lis pendens) against the property in the registry of deeds, which will effectively restrict the sale of the property until the legal issue is resolved.

In certain cases, the seller may not wish to enter into a binding contract by accepting the offer to purchase, while the real estate is delisted from the market. Here, the contract may be drafted using safe harbor language, clearly stating the limitation of obligations that are created through acceptance of the offer.

COMPETENCY *(M.G.L. c. 233. § 20)*

Capability

All the parties to a contract must possess the capacity and ability to understand the terms and conditions of the contract that they are agreeing to as well as the consequences of adhering and violating any of these.

For example, minor children, mentally challenged persons, animals and such other entities do not possess the capacity and ability to enter into a contract, hence any contracts involving them are considered void or voidable.

Although corporations are technically considered as legal fiction, under the law, they are deemed to be persons or individuals and hence fit to enter into contracts. For adults, statutes are established declaring their capacity to be parties to a contract as presumed. Hence any adult resisting contract enforcement on the basis of insufficient capacity to be bound owns the burden of persuasion with respect to capacity.

CONSENT (DURESS-NOTARY)

State laws usually require that a contract (purchase and sale agreement) must be signed by the grantor (seller) and the grantee (buyer) in the presence of two witnesses. The two witnesses are required to sign the contract document as an attestation of the signatures of the parties concerned. This is a formal declaration that the grantee is accepting the grantor's offer, including all the terms and conditions mentioned in the final contract (purchase and sale agreement) and is doing so voluntarily, without any kind of duress or pressure, and that the signatures are genuine, as acknowledged by the witnesses. Such a declaration is made in the presence of a notary public, who also signs the contract document and whose signature serves as a witness to the signing of the contract by the parties involved.

TERMINATION OF AN OFFER (M.G.L. C. 106. § 2-106)

On reading this section completely, you will understand;

- Why does an offer terminate on the death of the offeror?
- What happens to an offer when its time limit expires?
- What happens when an Offeror withdraws an offer?
- Why does an Offer terminate on Acceptance by the grantee?
- Why does an Offer terminate on revocation by the Offeree?
- What happens in case of a Counteroffer?

DEATH OF OFFEROR

Generally, the death or incapacitation of the offeror results in termination of the offer. The offeree cannot accept the offer if he or she has prior knowledge of the death of the offeror. In situations where the offeree accepts an offer while being ignorant about the death of the offeror, the contract may be considered valid depending on the type or contents of the offer. If the contract includes some personal element of the offeror, then such an offer gets disbanded on the death of the offeror.

In real estate, a purchase & sale signed by an owner is enforceable. The estate of the owner is required to complete the contract by executing and delivering a proper deed.

In case of death of the offeree, the offer becomes invalid.

TIME LIMIT

While making an offer, the offeror may include a duration or time period for which the offer is held valid. In such cases, if the offeree does not accept the offer within the specified time period then the offer is considered terminated.

WITHDRAWAL BY OFFEROR

An offeror may withdraw an offer prior to its acceptance by the offeree; however, such a revocation of the offer has to be communicated to the offeree.

If the offer is enclosed within an option, then such an offer cannot be revoked. If an offer is likely to result into a unilateral contract, then such an offer cannot be revoked after the offeree has started performing the promise.

ACCEPTANCE

An acceptance is a promise or action by an offeree indicating a willingness to adhere to the terms and conditions stated in an offer. It is also an acknowledgement by a drawee that binds him or her to the terms and conditions of a draft.

REVOCATION BY OFFEREE

An offer is considered to be terminated if it is rejected by the offeree. This means that the offeree is not agreeing to the terms and conditions specified in the offer by the offeror.

COUNTEROFFER

If an offeree does not agree, fully or partially, with the terms specified in an offer then he or she may either reject the offer completely or make a counter-offer to the offeror. A counter-offer may include terms from the original offer that are modified to suit the offeree or completely new terms that were not included in the original offer made by the offeror. Usually, when a counter-offer is generated, the original offer is killed and cannot be accepted in the future.

VALID/VOID/VOIDABLE

On reading this section completely, you will understand;

- What are the requirements for a deed to be held valid in Massachusetts?
- In what kind of situations is a deed considered void?
- Under what conditions does a deed become voidable?

Massachusetts Deed Validity Requirements

(See also Module I)

A new deed is made and handed out every time the title is transferred. Any existing estate of homestead gets terminated automatically, if the owner and his or her spouse, if any, convey the real property through a deed.

➢ A deed has to be created in writing and must include the necessary language expressing grant or conveyance of the real property

➢ The grantor must adhere to the same name used at the time of taking the title. If the grantor's name while taking the title originally was different, then both the current name and original name of the grantor are required to be included in the deed. For example, if any woman acquires property prior to marriage and then marries, her pre-marriage and post-marriage names, both, must be incorporated in the conveyance deed

➤ The grantor is required to be lawfully competent

➤ The grantee should be alive and distinctly identifiable. The grantee's full name and address must be contained in the deed. If there are two or more grantees, then the deed must classify the co-ownership type.

➤ The deed must distinctly indicate the grantor's intention to convey the title. Under Massachusetts law, inserting the word "grant" is adequate and use of this word does not imply any covenant

➤ The deed must state the total value of the purchase transaction. It must contain a consideration clause – for a fee or for love and affection.

➤ Every deed of unregistered land submitted for recording must necessarily contain the description of the property to be conveyed, in order to accurately and sufficient identify it. According to M.G.L. c. 183. § 6A, such descriptions must comprise references to previously recorded instruments or plans or those recorded along with the conveyance. M.G.L. c. 183, § 6 stipulates that the deed must state the street address (metes & bounds) of the concerned property, within the margin.

➤ Signature & Notarization

➤ The conveyance deed is considered to be effective when it is handed over to and accepted by the grantee or his or her agent

➤ A deed for registered land has to be acknowledged in order to be recorded. Only after the deed gets recorded, the old certificate of title will be replaced with a new one proving the conveyance. In case of unregistered land, notarizing a deed to evidence the conveyance is optional, but it becomes mandatory if the deed has to be recorded. Under Massachusetts law, notarizing a deed is not needed in order for it to be held valid. However, notarizing is mandatory in case it has to be recorded.

Note:

The title does not get transferred if a deed is recorded. The purpose of recording is simply to give intimation to the public or the world (constructive notice). The title is generally conveyed when the deed is delivered along with intent and acceptance.

Void

Voided contracts are unenforceable by either party. A contract to perform something illegal is void. In some states, entering into a contract on a Sunday and some national holidays may void a contract. In Massachusetts, contracts are valid whenever and wherever signed.

Voidable

A contract is considered voidable if any one of the parties involved possesses the option to terminate it. Contracts generally have a rescission clause for either of the parties in real estate. For example, a contract with a minor is considered voidable.

The age of majority in Massachusetts is 18. **(M.G.L. c. 231. § 85P)**

PURCHASE AND SALE AGREEMENT

On reading this section completely, you will understand;

- Why should a P&S agreement include the names of the parties involved?
- How is land described in a P&S agreement?
- What do price / consideration mean in a property transaction?
- What, when and how much about deposits related to property deals?
- The importance of dates in a property transaction.
- The significance of signatures of the parties involved in a property contract.

NAME OF PARTIES

The names and addresses of both, the Buyer and the Seller must be appropriately stated, in detail, in the purchase and sale agreement in order to make this document effectively binding on both the parties. The names and full details of the lawyers and real estate brokers are also usually included as a best practice.

DESCRIPTION OF LAND

Since a real estate contract requires an accurate description of the property to be transacted (bought and sold), correct information has to be stated in it. Usually it includes a reference to the record (book and page or the document number) of the existing owner's deed, at the Registry of Deeds.

PRICE/CONSIDERATION

The P&S agreement must include the total purchase price or consideration mutually agreed between the Buyer and the Seller. This document must also include all the other financial components such as the amount paid along with the offer-to-purchase (usually in the range of $500 - $1000), the deposit amount being paid with this P&S agreement (generally about 5%) and the balance amount that will be paid at the time of closing of the deal.

DEPOSIT (INCL. ESCROW)

Both the parties involved in the purchase and sale of a real property have to be clear and reach a mutual understanding about the entity that will hold any deposit funds and the procedure to be followed in case a dispute arises. All agreements have to be in writing and neither party should sign any agreement or make any payments until they are sure that all the terms have been clearly understood.

If the broker accepts money from the buyer then such payment has to be deposited in an escrow account within a short time. An escrow account is a bank account specifically maintained for the purpose of depositing and holding funds that belong to others. The money has to be retained in the escrow account until the successful completion or termination of the transaction. If the broker mixes the deposit received with his or her own funds, then it is an illegal act.

DATE

Important dates pertaining to the property sale transaction must be appropriately listed in the P&S agreement. These include the mortgage contingency date – the cut-off date for the buyer to acquire their mortgage commitment; the date on which the closing is scheduled and any other dates related to special conditions or important milestones. However, all the parties involved must remain flexible on the dates mentioned, especially the closing date since problems may arise causing delays in mortgage acquisition or title search examination etc.

SIGNATURES (M.G.L.C. 110G)

The Buyer and the Seller involved in the real estate sale transaction are required to sign the purchase and sale agreement document. Signing of the P&S is a proof of acceptance of the terms and conditions stated therein by both the parties and make the agreement legal, binding and enforceable.

Electronic signatures technology is rapidly gaining acceptance across the US and is implemented in Massachusetts too. Electronic signature software allows transmission of legally binding documents for obtaining signatures anytime, anywhere and through any device connected to the Internet.

Electronic signatures are held valid in contracts related to Massachusetts real estate.

For additional information, please see (M.G.L. c. 184. § 17A)

MISCELLANEOUS

On reading this section completely, you will understand;

- What is the Mass. Statute of Frauds with respect to a Written Purchase and Sale Agreement?
- What is an Equitable title and a Legal title to a property?
- What is the Right to Assign?

MASS. STATUTE OF FRAUDS - WRITTEN P & S (M.G.L.c. 259)

Under Massachusetts Contract Law, the Statute of Frauds requires specific contracts to be in writing so that they are enforceable. Mere compliance with all the key components of contract creation does not suffice. The statute that enumerates this requirement is known as the Statute of Frauds.

Such documents are usually related to sale, lease or mortgage of real estate; long term contracts with durations greater than one year from the date of drafting and with specific terms and conditions;

The original Statute of Frauds requires five types of contracts to be in writing, in order to be enforceable. These are;

1) Contracts that cannot be executed (or performed) within one year from the date of their creation.

2) Contracts where a Third Party stands surety to pay the debt of another party.

3) A Contract executor's promise to pay the debt pertaining to a decedent's real estate.

4) Contracts related to marriage.

5) Contracts involving real estate or property.

Contracts containing subject matter falling under any of the above categories have to be in writing, not oral, for them to have any legal validity. A Purchase and Sale Agreement (P&S) is a Contract related to property. Hence the P&S has to be in writing and cannot be simply oral in nature, for it to be legally enforceable. Other such Contracts include deeds, mortgages, easements, leases and deeds of trust etc.

However, an exception to this rule is a situation where a person promises to sell property to another and the buyer moves onto the property, pays a part of the consideration agreed upon, takes possession and makes significant improvements to it. In such cases, the Contract need not be in writing and it can be enforced through the 'Doctrine of Detrimental Reliance'. [Estoppel]

Pre-nuptial and collateral agreements and contracts involving sale of goods valued at over $500 are also categorized under the Statute of Frauds.

EQUITABLE VS LEGAL TITLE

Equitable title is one that is vested in a person who is deemed to be the owner of a property through application of equitable principles although the legal title may be vested in another person. Simply put, an equitable title is the right to acquire a legal title on fulfilling a certain obligation.

For example, in a lease option or rent-to-buy option, the tenant-buyer agrees to buy the property from the landlord-seller before the end of the lease term, at a pre-determined price. In this case, the tenant-buyer is said to possess the equitable title until the lease conditions are fulfilled and he or she purchases the property following which the legal title will be transferred to his or her name.

Legal title is the one that is vested with the current owner of the property, whose name is recorded with the county registry of deeds as the existing owner of a particular property. Legal title is the proof of lawful ownership of the property. Legal title may be conveyed by the property owner to another person through sale or will or such other legitimate means.

For example, the legal title to a property rests with the current owner, whose name appears in the grantee index at the office of the recorder of deeds, as the person who received the title from the grantor – the previous owner of the property – through a recorded deed transaction. And who holds the certificate of title with his or her name as the present owner.

In short, as per common law, an equitable title is the right to acquire complete ownership of a property while another person holds the legal title to the same property and a legal title is actual ownership of a real property.

RIGHT TO ASSIGN

The assignment of a right or obligation is a contractual phenomenon according to the law. The right to assign (prohibition against assignment) is commonly encountered in most property agreements, leases and related documents.

An assignment means the transfer of rights possessed by one party known as the 'assignor' to another party known as the 'assignee'. The legality of the assignment and the contract terms of the agreement executed between the parties form the basis of certain additional rights and liabilities that supplement the assignment. The assignment of rights encased in a contract generally transfers all the rights to the assignee to enjoy the benefits derived from the contract. Normally, the term 'assignment' is restricted to the transfer of intangible rights such as contractual rights and those related to property.

The law generally permits a right to assign unless an express prohibition is stated in the contract or lease. In cases where assignments are permitted, the assignor is not required to seek the consent of the other party to the contract. The assignor may simply assign the rights at any point of time; however, such assignment can neither adversely impact the duties of the other party nor reduce his or her chances of receiving complete performance. The assignor is generally held liable unless the other party has agreed to a contrary alternative.

In most jurisdictions, for the assignment to be considered valid, it has to occur in the present. Future rights cannot be assigned. The assignment confers only immediate rights and obligations.

Although no particular language is necessary to create an assignment, using the correct language is essential to avoid litigation later. An assignment is good as long as the assignor explicitly expresses his or her intent to assign specific contractual rights to the assignee.

BREACH OF CONTRACT (M.G.L. C. 259 - 260)

On reading this section completely, you will understand;

- What are the damages incurred and the consequences in case of a breach of contract?
- What is specific performance in relation to a breach of contract?
- Why and when is a deposit retained if a contract is breached?
- How is the right of rescission exercised in case of a breach of contract?

A contract is a promise that is legally enforceable. The promise could be for buying an item or delivering a service or rendering a job. If one of the parties involved breaks a promise, then the other party may sue it for breach of contract.

In other words, a breach of contract means retracting on a commitment or agreement, written or verbal, without a valid and lawful reason. Examples of breach of contract are, leaving a job incomplete; not making full payment or on scheduled time, for goods purchased or services availed; delivering incomplete orders or providing different items or of inferior quality; and such other acts.

DAMAGES

A breach of contract that erodes significant value from the wronged party is called a material breach and may warrant a lawsuit. A breach of contract that has very little impact on the value of the agreement is considered a minor breach and a lawsuit filed is unlikely to succeed.

To recover compensation for breach of contract, a party must adequately prove that their interests were harmed by the other party in some manner. This is termed as 'damages'. Damages may include not just monetary losses, but time lost too. Usually, the breaching party has to pay for all the expenses incurred as a consequence of the violation. Further, the breaching party may also have to pay punitive damages – punishment to the party for breach of contract. If the contract itself includes any terms or conditions for payment of charges to the wronged party by the offending party on the breach of contract, then such terms may also be fulfilled in addition to the compensation awarded by the court of law.

The offending party may be required to complete the contract terms or the wronged party may request the court to void the contract and restore it to the position it was in prior to entering the contract.

SPECIFIC PERFORMANCE

If a seller breaches or retracts from an oral promise made to a buyer, the buyer is entitled to specific performance even if the seller enters in to a contract with a third party for sale / lease of the property, as per the law.

In some circumstances it is unjust to allow the defaulting party to merely compensate the aggrieved party to the extent of the damages incurred. The court may issue an order of "specific performance", which requires that the contract be executed (performed). In certain situations, the court may order a party to fulfill his or her promise (order to "specific performance") or issue an order to a party to refrain from acting in a manner that would lead to breach of contract (an "injunction" order).

Both, "specific performance" and "injunction" are discretionary remedies, mostly originating from equity. Neither is considered a right and in most cases, the court does not generally order specific performance.

RETAIN DEPOSIT

In Massachusetts, the amount that a property buyer usually deposits along with the offer to purchase form is $500 - $1000. On signing the purchase and sale agreement (P&S), the buyer deposits an additional 5% of the total consideration, agreed upon with the seller, in the escrow account.

Buyer's Breach of Contract

There are instances where the buyer wants to terminate the property contract and exit. There could be various reasons for such a decision on the part of the buyer such as dissatisfaction after a home inspection, detection of radon or mold, or any other unanticipated problem with the real estate. The buyer usually includes contingencies in the contract for the reasons that he or she may wish to terminate the contract. In such scenarios, there will not be any problem and the buyer will get a refund of the full deposit amount. However, in some cases, the buyer may want to back out from the property contract after the lapse of all the contingency dates. In such cases, the seller is entitled to retain the money deposited in the escrow account. The seller may also sue the buyer for damages, but it is observed in most cases of property contract breaches that the seller's damages are limited to the deposit amount.

Seller's Breach of Contract

In case a seller wishes to retract from a property contract the consequences could be severe. In Massachusetts, an offer to purchase property is 'binding' on both parties. Hence, in case of breach of contract by the seller, the buyer may sue the seller for specific performance and compel the seller to sell his or her home.

The seller may have genuine reasons for deciding to breach a real estate contract such as remorse due to unavailability of the house that he or she intended to buy or some health problem that may crop up unexpectedly or a number of other such reasons. This can make selling a problematic issue before the transaction is completed.

In such a scenario, the first thing that the seller should do is to inform his or her listing agent. The seller's decision to retract from a contract will make a lot of people unhappy such as the seller's agent, the buyer and his or her agent and attorneys from both sides involved, if any, in the deal.

The seller must prepare to face any or a combination of the following situations;

> Release the buyer's escrow deposit along with accumulated interest.

> Reimburse the buyer's out-of-pocket expenses incurred in the course of the transaction such as mortgage application fee, inspection costs, attorney expenses, mortgage lock-in fees etc.

> Bear the interim housing expenses, in case the buyer has already sold his or her home with the expectation of moving in to the seller's home.

> Bear the increased mortgage rates incurred by the buyer, if the rates have changed during the course of the contract.

Although some buyers may be nice and let the seller excuse himself / herself from the contract with just a return of escrow deposit, not every buyer will be so kind. In such situations, the seller should look for a competent real estate attorney who can negotiate the best terms with the buyer or their attorney.

RIGHT OF RESCISSION *(M.G.L. c. 259, § 1)*

If a specific mention of the type of deed is not included in the deed document, then it is considered to be a general warranty deed.

If the grantor(s) (seller) breaches any of the warranties that have been conveyed through the deed, then the grantee(s) (buyer) may choose to rescind the contract and obtain refund of the purchase price already paid or retain the property and sue the grantor(s) for damages incurred due to the breach of the covenant.

Deeds (M.G.L. c. 183)

On reading this section completely, you will understand;

- Who is a grantor and grantee in a property deed?
- What is the county registry of deeds?
- What is a book and page reference?
- What is the difference between Quitclaim, Warranty and Special Warranty deeds?

Grantor/Grantee

A grantor is the owner of a property, who wishes to sell his or her land to an interested buyer in exchange of a certain consideration. The grantor executes the deed and conveys the property to another person. A grantor can be more than one person, or a corporation, partnership firm, limited liability company (LLC) or such other entity.

A grantee is the buyer of the property. It is a person who is interested in purchasing a property from a prospective seller by paying a certain consideration as mutually agreed with the grantor. The grantee receives the title to the property from the grantor. A grantee can be more than one person, a corporation, partnership firm, LLC or such other entity.

All the records that indicate ownership or title to different properties located within a county are indexed on the names of the grantors and grantees. There are separate indexes maintained in chronological order of the grantors' names (grantor index) and grantees' names (grantee index) at the county registry of deeds.

County Registry of Deeds

The titles to all land or real estate located within the geographical bounds of a county and all property instruments such as deeds, mortgages, easements, leases and court orders are recorded in a register at the county registry of deeds. This country registry of deeds is usually the elected office of the recorder of deeds or registrar of titles and is also called the 'county recorder'.

The records registered with the county registry of deeds are public records, which can be accessed by interested parties to verify the title and ownership to a particular property before doing a property transaction.

Registry of Deeds Websites

Barnstable
http://www.barnstabledeeds.org/

Berkshire Middle
http://berkshiremiddledeeds.com/

Berkshire North
http://www.sec.state.ma.us/rod/rodbrknth/brknthidx.htm

Berkshire South
http://www.sec.state.ma.us/rod/rodbrksth/brksthidx.htm

Bristol Fall River
https://www.fallriverdeeds.com/

Bristol North
http://www.tauntondeeds.com/

Bristol South
http://www.newbedforddeeds.com/

Dukes
http://www.masslandrecords.com/Dukes/

Essex South
http://www.salemdeeds.com/

Essex North
http://www.sec.state.ma.us/rod/rodnrthessex/nrthessexidx.htm

Franklin
http://www.sec.state.ma.us/rod/rodfranklin/franklinidx.htm

Hampden
http://www.registryofdeeds.co.hampden.ma.us/

Hampshire
http://www.sec.state.ma.us/rod/rodhamp/hampidx.htm

Middlesex North
http://www.lowelldeeds.com/

Middlesex South
http://www.sec.state.ma.us/rod/rodmidsth/midsthidx.htm

Plymouth
http://plymouthdeeds.org/

Suffolk
http://www.suffolkdeeds.com/

Worcester
http://www.worcesterdeeds.com/

Worcester North
http://www.sec.state.ma.us/rod/rodnw/nwidx.htm

BOOK AND PAGE REFERENCE

The details of the title to each property or pertaining to a deed transaction are recorded in a register (book) at the office of the registry of deeds. Each such recorded is assigned a book and page number for easy identification and searching, when it is required to be accessed sometime in the future.

QUITCLAIM VS WARRANTY VS SPECIAL WARRANTY

Quitclaim Deed (M.G.L. c. 183, § 11)

In Massachusetts, a quitclaim deed, unlike its equivalent used elsewhere across the country, is comparable to the special warranty deed commonly in use in most other states. The quitclaim deed used in Massachusetts offers the buyer two quitclaim or limited covenants when the deed is delivered. These are;

3. The grantor has not created any encumbrances over the land apart from those particularly expressed in the deed. Contrary to a special warranty deed used in most states, the quitclaim encompasses only encumbrances created by the grantor. It excludes other pre-existing encumbrances like easements, municipal limitations or restrictions, rights of way and such others.

4. The quitclaim deed provides the grantee the same force and effect as that of a deed in fee simple. It the grantor and his or her heirs' obligation to warrant and defend the grantee by countering any claims and demands, only for the period that the property is under the grantor's ownership.

Warranty Deed (M.G.L. c. 183, § 10)

In Massachusetts, a warranty deed is analogous to a general warranty deed used in most states across the country. A warranty deed offers the buyer four warranty covenants when the deed is delivered. These are;

5. The grantor is the owner of the property in fee simple

6. The property concerned is free of any encumbrances besides those particularly described in the deed

7. The grantor holds the right for conveying the property to the grantee, his or her heirs and assigns

8. It is the duty of the grantor and his or her heirs to warrant and defend the title by countering any legal claims or demands from any other person arising before and until the grantor's lawful ownership of the property.

Special Warranty Deed

A special warranty deed, as opposed to a general warranty deed, limits the grantor's liability by warranting only the explicitly stated contents of the deed. Its effect is practically similar to a quitclaim deed. In case of a special warranty deed, the grantor limits the warranty on the title transferred to the grantee by including covenants that cover any such claims arising by, through, from or under the grantor and not any predecessors to the title. The grantor warrants defending the title only against his or her own actions and omissions and not against any title defects that may have existed prior to the grantor acquiring ownership of the property. In other words, the grantor warrants that no act was committed by him or her to impair the title to the property during the time period that he or she held it.

In contrast to the general warranty deed, the special warranty deed is less protective of the grantee (buyer), and hence, grantors always prefer the latter over the former for conveyance of real estate interests. The decision of opting for either of these two deed types depends on which party is in a better position to search and identify the title defects and the allocation of the title defect risks between the parties. Though grantors (sellers) are in a stronger position than the grantees (buyers), to identify and obtain information about the title defects, the grantors may not be interested in conducting extensive research about the historical chain of title of the property in question.

Consequently, most parties depend on title insurance, which covers various types of losses likely to be incurred if title defects are later discovered. Most title insurance companies conduct a thorough search of the relevant title records to ascertain presence of any title defects, prior to issuing policies. If a purchaser of real property succeeds in obtaining title insurance then he or she need not be much concerned about accepting a special warranty deed from a seller.

Special warranty deeds, similar to general warranty deeds, must include the correct language e.g. 'conveys and specially warrants'. Special warranty deeds are usually preferred by corporations or such entities who want to avoid the liability that comes with a general warranty deed.

ELEMENTS OF A DEED (M.G.L. c. 183)

On reading this section completely, you will understand;

- How all the parties involved in a property transaction are identified in the deed document?
- What is the granting clause with respect to a deed?
- What the meaning of 'Consideration' in a property deed?
- How is the transfer of rights explained in a deed?
- What is legal description of property and how is it described in a deed?
- What are the requirements for proper execution of a deed?
- Why must a deed be recorded at the registry of deeds in order to make it valid and effective?

Certain legal requirements must be met to qualify for valid conveyance by deed: title transfer from grantor (seller or vendor) to grantee (buyer or vendee).

1. Identification of all parties
2. Granting clause
3. Consideration
4. Legal description
5. Proper execution
6. Delivery & acceptance

IDENTIFICATION OF ALL PARTIES (ET UX, ET AL)

All the parties involved in executing a deed have to be explicitly named and their full details included in a deed for proper identification. The deed must include the full names of the grantor(s) and grantee(s) involved in the execution of the deed. Their address, phone numbers and other relevant details are also usually included in the deed document.

If the grantor(s) or grantee(s) are husband and wife, then the full name of the husband – as the first grantor or grantee - is mentioned first, followed by "et ux" - an abbreviation for "et uxor" meaning "and wife" - in the deed. 'Et' means 'and' and 'Uxor' means 'wife' in Latin. The name of the wife need not be mentioned in such cases, for example, John Sanders et ux. If the wife is the first grantor then the expression "et vir" is used, for example, Mary Alden et vir. Here "vir' means 'husband' in Latin. In both these cases, the grantor(s) or grantee(s) have to be spouses.

If the grantor(s) or grantee(s) are more than one person, especially a large group of persons and not necessarily spouses, then the full name of the first grantor or grantee (and optionally second grantor or grantee) is mentioned followed by "et al" meaning "and others" in the deed. Here 'al' is an abbreviation for "others", which includes multiple persons and both genders. 'Alii' represents masculine (plural), 'aliae' represents feminine (plural) and 'alia' represents neuter (plural). The full names and details of all the grantor(s) or grantee(s) need not be stated explicitly.

GRANTING CLAUSE

This clause in a deed lists the grantor(s) (transferor or seller) and the grantee(s) (transferee or buyer) involved in the property transaction and specifies that the property in question is being transferred by the grantor(s) to the grantee(s).

The granting clause generally mentions the consideration that the grantee(s) is / are paying for the land, however, this is not to be mandatorily included in the deed. Consideration is not required for completing a property transfer.

The purpose of the consideration being stated in the deed document is to bestow the grantee(s) with a "bona-fide purchaser" status, which is necessary for protecting the grantee(s) from repossession of the property by the grantor(s) or against claims on the property by a third party later on.

In any case, a deed executed without mention of any consideration is still legally binding on all the parties involved.

The granting clause must list both the parties involved in the property transaction. However, the parties may not necessarily be listed by name in the deed. A clear description that eliminates any doubt about the identity of the parties usually suffices.

For example, Joe and Susan have one daughter, Emily. Steve, a friend of Joe and Susan wishes to sell a piece of property to Emily. If Steve executes a deed to the property in favor of Emily, the deed must either provide the full name and details of Emily or must describe her in such a manner that clearly identifies Emily, leaving no doubt whatsoever. If the deed states that the property purchaser is the only daughter of Joe and Susan, then that description of Emily is considered sufficient to make the deed valid.

CONSIDERATION

Consideration is the value given by the grantee to the grantor in exchange for the property conveyance. This value can be in terms of the price (money) given or goods or services or any such item or element that has certain worth associated with it or a combination of any of these. In some cases, the exact consideration given by the grantee is stated in the deed, while in other cases only a statement of basic consideration is included in the deed along with a mention of good and valuable consideration.

EXPLANATION OF RIGHTS TRANSFERRED

Every deed must include a mention of what type of deed it is and an explicit explanation of all the rights transferred from the grantor(s) to the grantee(s). If the deed type is not mentioned it is considered to be a general warranty deed.

In case of a Quitclaim deed, the transferor transfers all of his or her rights to the property to the transferee. This has to be explicitly stated using the right legal language. Once this deed is executed the transferor has not right whatsoever to the property. However, this deed does not warrant the validity of the title or protect the buyer from claims on the property from a third party.

In a General Warranty deed, the grantor not only transfers the title to the property to the grantee, but also has to explicitly convey five special guarantees, known as 'covenants', through this type of deed. These are;

> ➢ The grantor guarantees that he or she is the lawful owner of the land / property being conveyed to the grantee.

> ➢ The grantor promises that he or she possesses the power and authority (right to convey) to sell and transfer the property to the grantee.

> ➢ The grantor promises to the grantee that the property being conveyed is free from any easements, liens, mortgages or any such encumbrances.

> ➢ The grantor explicitly states that he or she will protect the grantee from claims of superior title from a third party and compensate the grantee if such third party successfully takes the title or any portion of it.

> The grantor states in the deed that he or she will transfer a clear title to the grantee and help in ironing out any imperfections that may exist such as a mortgage on the property at the time of the transfer.

In case of a Special Warranty deed, the grantor explicitly assures the grantee through the deed that he or she is the lawful owner of the property and provides the same guarantees as in General Warranty deed. However, these guarantees are with respect to the defects that arose only during his or her possession of the property and not prior that, when the property was in possession of any of the previous owners.

Similarly, in any other type of deed the rights being transferred have to be clearly stated and a proper explanation provided for the grantee's understanding and facilitate enforcement of the deed.

LEGAL DESCRIPTION (METES & BOUNDS, LOT & BLOCK, GOV'T SURVEY)

Real Estate Legal Descriptions

Legal description denotes the written description of a property and other specific information that helps identify a piece of property. The intent of parties to a property transaction may be dishonored unless the legal description of the land in question accurately locates it. Each legal description must include the name of the county or parish and its subdivisions, if any, such as a judicial district, within which the concerned property is located. The most common methods of describing land are;

> Fractional designation
> Metes and Bounds
> Courses and Distances
> Subdivision lot
> Name Designation
> Portion of a tract
> Blanket
> Reference

Some of these are explained below.

In Massachusetts, land is described using a concept called 'full legal description'. This consists of three components;

1. Street or nominated address of the property concerned. In a deed, a street address, by itself, is not considered as an adequate description of a tract of land and is not accepted as the sole description.

2. Metes and Bounds Description – This describes the length and location of the different boundaries of a piece of property, including the ownership details of the strips of land adjacent to it. For example, the boundaries may be natural or artificial such as roads, streets or creek and the adjacent land ownership may be determined as John on the West and Susan on the South. A description that includes the size of the piece of land and three of the four sides surrounding it is usually sufficient. Many lawyers and surveyors consider the metes-and-bounds description same as the courses-and-distances description explained below.

3. Reference Description – This is a pointer to another recorded document that provides greater details of the location, size and shape of the real estate. Examples of this could be a previous deed reference (book, page and date); plan or plat number in the Registry of Deeds, or a certificate number obtained from the Land Court records.

Usually, each survey or full legal description starts with a monument, often referred to as a 'benchmark', which is a static, permanent marker. The description then progresses around the property, from one monument to another. In Massachusetts, monuments are typically iron pipes, trees, boulders, buildings, granite blocks, telephone poles etc. Monuments that appear fixed and permanent are often moved, changed or lost over a period of time. This renders a current survey nearly mandatory in most property transactions, making it necessary to find out the local body qualified to conduct such a survey. Although not mandatory, without a current survey, the buyer fails to understand what he or she is actually buying. In the case of a property being sub-divided, a survey is essential and a plat has to be obtained. The top of the plat is considered to represent the north direction and has to be indicated by an arrow.

Fractional Designation

The fractional designation is based on the rectangular system of surveying accepted and implemented in the United States in 1785. This system establishes a series of baselines and meridians - permanent reference points (or 'monuments'). The surveyors actually placed a fixed group of boundary markers at all sections.

The baseline is a line extending from east to the west from a pre-determined point on the principal meridian at an approximate right angle to the principal meridian. The principal meridian is a line extending from the north to the south from a specific point on the baseline through a certain tract of the country that is to be surveyed. The survey of such a tract is conducted by referring to the baseline and the principal meridian.

Numbering is done for the ranges situated on the east and west of the principal meridian and for the townships situated on the north and south of the baseline. By establishing township corners along these two lines, the tracts of land are divided using lines intersecting the true north and south at 90° (right angle) to create townships that are six miles square. The townships are numbered in progression on the north and south of the baseline and on the east and west of the principal meridian. The townships are divided into 36 sections. Each section is one square mile and consists of nearly 640 acres. The section on the north-east is numbered one and the numbering then progresses to the subsequent sections in the west direction till that end of the township and then turns towards the east and so on, alternating directions at every end of the township till the count reaches 36.

Each section of the township is further subdivided in four quarter sections of about 160 acres each, by running one line from north to south and another line from east to west intersecting at the center of the section or by joining the four quarter-corner points of the section. Each quarter-section of 160 acres can be further sub-divided using the same method described above in to quarter-sections of 40 acres each and so on.

Since the earth's surface is curved, not flat, all the townships do not equal precisely six square miles and consequentially, each section does not measure up to an exact 640 acres. In most states of the US, the county is considered the basic unit and hence the need for a reference to a specific baseline or principal meridian is eliminated, for a complete description.

One Section is 640 Acres - One Mile by One Mile (5280' x 5280')

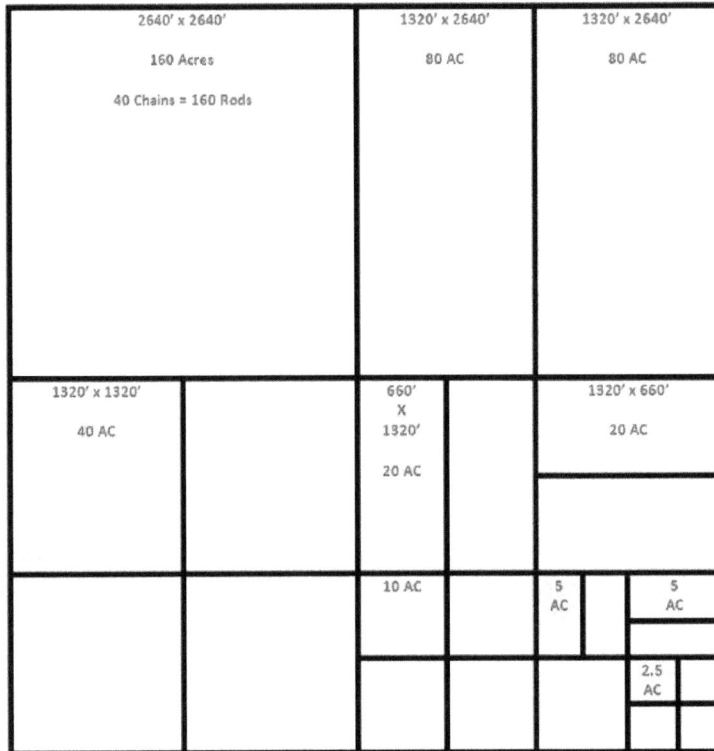

2640' x 2640' 160 Acres 40 Chains = 160 Rods		1320' x 2640' 80 AC		1320' x 2640' 80 AC
1320' x 1320' 40 AC		660' X 1320' 20 AC		1320' x 660' 20 AC
		10 AC		5 AC / 5 AC / 2.5 AC

Rectangular Survey System

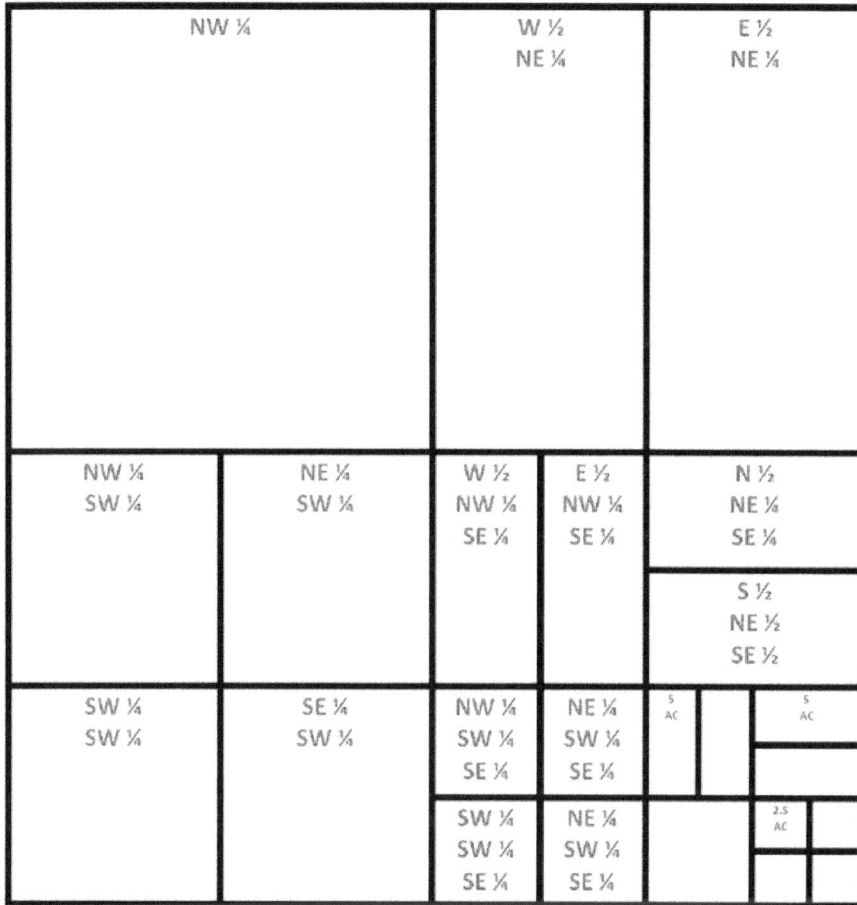

NW ¼

W ½ NE ¼

E ½ NE ¼

NW ¼ SW ¼

NE ¼ SW ¼

W ½ NW ¼ SE ¼

E ½ NW ¼ SE ¼

N ½ NE ¼ SE ¼

S ½ NE ½ SE ½

SW ¼ SW ¼

SE ¼ SW ¼

NW ¼ SW ¼ SE ¼

NE ¼ SW ¼ SE ¼

5 AC

5 AC

SW ¼ SW ¼ SE ¼

NE ¼ SW ¼ SE ¼

2.5 AC

Metes and Bounds

Metes-and-bounds descriptions identify land by reference to (1) natural or artificial boundaries such as streets, roads, or creeks, or (2) the land of adjoining owners, such as Smith on the south, Williams on the west. The description must establish all sides of the property by either specifically identifying what constitutes the respective boundary or providing enough information to calculate the size and shape of the land from the boundaries given. Therefore, a description that includes the size of the tract and three of the four sides will suffice.[1]

Many lawyers and surveyors refer to a courses-and-distances description as a metes-and-bounds description.

Lot & Block Survey System

The lot and block survey system is a method for locating and identifying land, specifically 'lots', in densely populated urban metropolitan areas and suburbs. It is also known as the Recorded Plat Survey System or the Recorded Map Survey System. This survey system was widely adopted and implemented in the 19th century in the USA, when cities expanded into the surrounding farming zones. The owners of large pieces of land created plats and subdivided their land into groups of smaller lots for selling to prospective buyers. Such a subdivision survey plan was recorded with a record keeper and its map became the legal description for the lots included in the subdivision.

The lot and block survey system starts with a large piece of land, which is usually described by one of the above mentioned survey systems such as the 'metes and bounds' system or 'public land survey system' etc. A subdivision survey is conducted for dividing the original piece of land and creating a plat map. Such subdivision surveys also use the metes and bounds survey system to demarcate individual lots within the larger land tract. Each lot defined on the plat map is assigned a number or a letter as an identifier mark. Then the plat map is recorded officially with a government body such as recorder of deeds or a city engineer. This plan is deemed as the legal description of all the lots within the subdivision. A simple reference to the independent lot and the record of the map constitutes the proper legal description.

A legal description under the lot and block survey system identifies;

> The individual lot.

> The block within which the lot is situated, if applicable.

> A reference / pointer to a platted subdivision or its phase.

> A page / volume number to identify the cited plat map.

> A description of the official recording place of the map (e.g. recorded with recorder of deeds).

For example, using the lot and block system, a legal description of a two and half acres property may read as Lot 4, Block 1 of the North subdivision plat recorded in map book 19, page 7 in the office of the recorder of deeds. Full technical details pertaining to the legal description of the property are included in the recorded plat map, hence reproducing them in a deed or any other legal description becomes unnecessary.

Courses and Distances

This is an ancient method of describing land. In this type of description, a definite or fixed start point is mandatorily required. From the start point a line is drawn to another point covering a certain distance. From there, the line is extended a third point some distance away and so on, until the line reaches and terminates in to the start point.

Signed

A deed must be signed by all the grantors, if more than one, mentioned in it. All such grantors must be aged at least 18 years or more and must be of sound mind. The signature of all the grantors in the appropriate place is mandatory for the deed to be held as valid conveyance, although the grantee(s) may be exempted from signing it.

Sealed

State laws usually require that the deed must be signed by the grantor in the presence of a witness. This is a formal declaration that the grantor is doing so voluntarily and the signature is genuine, acknowledged by the witnesses. Such a declaration is required to be made in front of a notary public, who also has to sign the deed document and whose signature is deemed as a witness to the grantor's signing. *Note: Notarization is not required for the validity of a deed. It is not however acceptable for public recording unless the signature is notarized.*

Delivered

In order to be effective, the deed has to be delivered by the grantor(s) and accepted by the grantee(s). Although there is no formal process, event or ceremony specified for delivery, the grantor must explicitly express his or her intent to transfer the title to the property. For this, the grantor(s) may either personally deliver the deed to the grantee(s) or arrange to deliver through a third party such as the grantor's attorney or through mail. A deed comes into effect on its date of delivery, unless specified otherwise by legislation.

Acceptance of a deed by the grantee(s) may not necessarily be expressed through words or in writing. Merely retaining it or obtaining mortgage against it is considered sufficient expression of acceptance by the grantee(s).

The recording process for a deed or such other instrument starts when it is submitted at the office of the country recorder or the registry of deeds. Recording of the deed is necessary for it to be held valid and effective.

Valid-Signed, Sealed, Delivered

A deed is considered 'valid' when it is;

- ✓ Signed by the grantor(s) and not necessarily by the grantee(s) and preferably at least two independent witnesses.

- ✓ Sealed means the signatures of the parties involved (grantor(s) and grantee(s)), and preferably the witnesses, have to be done in the presence of a public notary, who also signs the deed as an attestation that the grantor(s) signed the deed voluntarily and was / were not done under any kind of pressure or duress.

- ✓ Delivered to the grantee(s) by the grantor(s), either personally (physically) or through his or her attorney or through regular mail as an indication of his or her intent to transfer the title. Receiving and retaining the deed by the grantee is considered an indication of acceptance. The deed comes into effect on its date of delivery.

Fully Effective-Recorded-Acknowledged-Notarized

For a deed to be considered fully effective, it must be;

- ✓ Recorded – the deed is submitted to the county recorder's office. Photocopies of the entire document are obtained for duplication. One such copy is inserted at the appropriate place in the official book of records currently in use. The book and page reference are noted. The original deed document is returned to the registering party. Once the deed is recorded, it is deemed that all the parties involved have knowledge of its existence and contents as per the legislation of 'constructive notice', even if they have not physically seen the recorded deed.

- ✓ Acknowledged – when the grantor(s) signs the deed in the presence of a public notary, it is considered that the signature(s) of the grantor(s) is / are genuine and done voluntarily, not under duress. Such a formal declaration by a grantor(s) in the presence of an authorized public officer is called an acknowledgement.

- ✓ Notarized – The deed is said to be notarized if the grantor(s) sign in front of the public notary, who, in turn, signs the deed and puts his or her seal as an authentication of the genuineness and willingness of the grantor(s)' signature and intent to transfer the title.

TORRENS SYSTEM - LAND COURT, CERTIFICATE OF TITLE, LOW BOOK & PAGE

On reading this section completely, you will understand;

- What is a Torrens System of property registration?
- What is the significance of a Land Court?
- What is the meaning of Certificate of Title and why is it required?
- What is a low book and page reference?

Title recording systems have been a great means of recording, maintaining and accessing details of real estate ownership. In the US, the deed to a real estate is generally recorded in the county within which the property is located, at the county recorder's office. An alternative system for registration of titles to land is the Torrens system, which differs significantly from the traditional 'abstract' system and goes beyond simple recording of deeds.

In the Torrens system, the real estate deed is not recorded in the county, instead the title to the real estate is registered. In the abstract system, the evidence of the title is the abstract, while in the Torrens system the 'title' is the certificate of title itself.

LAND COURT

The registration process involves a court procedure where an Examiner of Title is appointed by a court for reviewing the parcel of land / property. If the title is found to be good after examination, the court issues a 'Certificate of Title'.

When a property owner first applies for a certificate of title in the Torrens system, a title search or examination is conducted, a court hearing is then held and finally a decree is issued confirming the title and ordering registration. This process is similar to that in a land court and recording of deeds with the registrar of deeds.

CERTIFICATE OF TITLE

A 'Certificate of Title' is a legal document confirming that the legal title to the concerned property is held by the certificate holder. It includes the name of the registered owner(s), a description of the real estate and entries pertaining to all restrictions, mortgages, conditions, liens, easements and any other encumbrances against the property title. It is considered as a valid proof against any claims that were undeclared or unrecorded during registration of the title.

Once the registration process is completed and a certificate of title is issued to the property owner, the property can be conveyed by executing deeds, submitting the previous certificate of title for cancellation and issuance of a new certificate of title to the new owner.

The title registered as per the Torrens system is generally guaranteed and marketable, rendering title insurance unnecessary and vastly reducing the time required for researching the title status during subsequent conveyances.

LOT BOOK AND PAGE

The land register is the center point of the Torrens system of land registration. During first-time registration of any parcel of land under the Torrens system, each parcel is allotted a unique number, known as a 'folio' that identifies the parcel of land by referencing a registered plan. The folio is actually derived by combining the details of the book and the page of the land register, on which the details of the land are recorded. Further transfer of ownership of such land is registered through change of record in the land register. The accuracy of this register is guaranteed by the state, which compensates such persons whose rights are violated by any administrative error.

The Torrens system was originally created by Sir Robert Torrens (1814 – 1884) for the purpose of maintaining and managing a ship registry in Australia, which was reliable, simple, suitable, fast and low cost.

MASS. TAX STAMPS - $2.28/$500 SELL PRICE--SELLER EXPENSE (M.G.L. c. 64D)

On reading this section completely, you will understand;

- What are Massachusetts tax stamps?
- What are the applicable tax rates on deed transfers?
- What happens in case of non-payment of such excise tax on a sale transaction?

In the commonwealth of Massachusetts, an excise tax is levied on all transactions involving the sale of a property (home). The current tax rate applicable is $4.56 / 1000 or $2.28 / $500 (M.G.L. c. 64D, § 1). This tax is levied in the form of 'Stamps' of the required amount that have to be affixed on the deed document. The person signing the deed (usually the 'seller') is responsible for paying the assessed tax (M.G.L. c. 64D, § 2).

For example, when a property is sold for a consideration of $500,000, the tax applicable on that transaction will be $2.28 x 1000 amounting to a total cost of $2280. This is amongst the largest expenses incurred while selling a property in Massachusetts, apart from the real estate commission that is required to be paid.

In case of non-payment of the tax applicable on the real estate transfer deed, a lien arises (after demand), however, such a lien is imposed on the seller's remaining property and not on the property transferred.

Further, failure to affix the appropriate amount of, or any, stamps on the deed document does not impact the validity of the deed (M.G.L. c. 64D, § 6A).

TITLE SEARCH (M.G.L. c. 185.)

On reading this section completely, you will understand;

- What are Grantor / Grantee Indices?
- What is a Chain of Title?
- What is an Abstract of Title?

GRANTORS/GRANTEES INDEX

Grantors / Grantees Index is a generic term for two separate lists of real estate transfer transactions maintained in an alphabetical order on the basis of last names of the parties involved in the property transfer. One of the lists is the grantor index – an alphabetical listing of the sellers (grantors) and the other list is the grantee index – an alphabetical listing of the buyers (grantees).

Each index is maintained by an official called the 'Recorder of Deeds' (also known as the 'County Recorder'). Transfer transactions are not mandatorily listed in alphabetical order, but often found to be listed in chronological order of the first letter of the last names of the party concerned. For example, in the grantors' index the entries are listed in alphabetical order of the grantors' last names. In each transaction entry the grantee's (buyer's) name is listed next, along with other details such as property location, volume and page number referring to full text of the deed or instrument where the transfer description is recorded. Similarly, the grantees' index includes all the details in the same manner.

In modern times, the online deeds recording system also includes all the information listed in a similar way, making it easier to search for specific records in both types of systems. Tracking historical transactions is also easier, since the current owner is the grantee and the previous owner, who transferred the property to the current owner, is listed as the grantor.

CHAIN OF TITLE

Chain of title is the sequential record of the history of transfers of the property title. The 'chain' extends in reverse order from the current owner to the original owner of the real estate, with the names of all the intermediate owners in between. In certain transactions, where ownership documents are vital, reconstructing the chain of title is necessary. In order to enable this, a record of the property title documents is generally maintained by the registry office.

In the real estate domain, the chain of title has substantial significance. In most cases, insurance companies issue the title insurance on the basis of the chain of title to the property at the time of transfer. Sometimes, insurance companies maintain their own private databases for tracking real estate titles apart from the official records. In certain cases, but not always, the chain of title is ascertained by an abstract to title, which is attested by an attorney.

ABSTRACT OF TITLE

An abstract of title is the abridged version of the history of the title to a specific parcel of property. It comprises of the summary of the original grant and all the conveyances and encumbrances related to the property, thereafter, along with a certificate from the abstractor regarding the completeness and accuracy of the history. In most of the US states, the abstract of title provides the raw data for preparing the title insurance policy for the parcel of real estate in question, with the exception of a few states.

CHAPTER 4

KEY TERMS

Listing	Grantor Deed	Grantee Deed
Mortgage Note	Discount Rate	Financing Clause
Real Estate Cycle	Balloon Mortgage	Construction Loan
Fannie Mae	Ginnie Mae	Freddie Mac
Second Mortgage	TILA	Equity

CHAPTER 4 LEARNING OBJECTIVES

- What are the key steps in a real estate cycle?
- What is a Listing?
- Why and how to qualify buyers?
- How to prepare for and conduct 'showing' of the property to prospective buyers?
- What is a Purchase & Sale Agreement and its significance?
- What are the wide variety of financing options that the buyer can choose from?
- What are the key stages of 'closing' and the pass papers (all important documents) that have to be signed by the parties involved in the property transaction?
- What are the steps involved prior to and while making a mortgage application?
- What are the three key parameters that banks scrutinize prior to approving a loan for purchasing property?
- What is the purchase and sale financing clause?
- What are the different types of finance / loan lending institutions?
- What is Federal Savings & Loan?
- What are commercial banks and their functions?
- What are mutual savings banks and their business?
- What are cooperative banks and their role in mortgage financing?
- What are credit unions and their area of operations?
- What role do mortgage companies play in mortgage financing?
- How are life insurance companies involved with property mortgages?
- What are the benefits of obtaining loans from private lenders?
- What is a Discount rate?
- What does Prime rate mean?
- What are mortgage rates?
- What is the meaning of Discounts or Points with respect to mortgage financing?
- How are buydowns beneficial as a mortgage financing method?
- What is a Grantor / Grantee Deed?
- What is a Mortgagor / Mortgagee Deed?
- What is a Mortgage Note?
- What are the different types of mortgages and how are they beneficial to the property buyer?
- What is a conventional mortgage?
- What is a Veterans Administration (VA) mortgage?
- What is a FHA loan and its key features?
- What is MGIC and the type of loan that it offers?
- How does a 'direct reduction' type of mortgage work?

- What is a 'construction' loan and where is it useful?
- What is a blanket mortgage and its characteristics?
- What is a 'package' loan and its use?
- How does a 'demand/open' loan work?
- Why is 'purchase money' mortgaging a good option?
- What is a 'junior / second' mortgage?
- What is the meaning of 'open end' mortgage?
- What are 'wraparound' mortgages?
- How does a 'variable rate' mortgage help in buying a property?
- How does 'balloon mortgage' benefit a property buyer?
- How and with whom is a 'shared equity' mortgage shared?
- What are the consequences of 'negative amortization'?
- What are 'equity loans'?
- What are the key differences between Primary and Secondary mortgage markets?
- What is Fannie Mae and its significance?
- What is Freddie Mac and its link to mortgage markets?
- What is Ginnie Mae and how is it different from the other two?
- What is the Truth-in-Lending Act (TILA) or Regulation Z?
- What businesses are covered under its purview?
- What are the mandatory disclosures under TILA?
- What is the 'right of rescission' under TILA and when does it apply?
- What are the advertising regulations specified by TILA?
-

FINANCING/MORTGAGES

REAL ESTATE CYCLE

On reading this section completely, you will understand;

- What are the key steps in a real estate cycle?
- What is a Listing?
- Why and how to qualify buyers?
- How to prepare for and conduct 'showing' of the property to prospective buyers?
- What is a Purchase & Sale Agreement and its significance?
- What are the wide variety of financing options that the buyer can choose from?
- What are the key stages of 'closing' and the pass papers (all important documents) that have to be signed by the parties involved in the property transaction?

LISTING

(M.G.L. c. 9. § 26D) Listing of the property that its owner wishes to sell is the first step in the real estate cycle. Although the seller has the option to sell the property on his or her own, it has several limitations and listing the property with a real estate agent is the best and often preferred option.

A listing contract or agreement is established between the real estate broker or their agent and the seller(s) (owner) of the property empowering the broker to offer the piece of real estate for sale on the owner's behalf.
The key components of the listing agreement are;

- ➢ The starting and termination dates

- ➢ The list price of the sale offer

- ➢ The broker's compensation – flat fee or percentage of sales price or any other form of charges

- ➢ The terms and conditions for payment of brokerage fee by the seller

- ➢ Authorizing the broker to liaise with other brokers, agents or the buyer's agents and specific compensation for such brokers who procure a buyer

> ➢ Authorizing the broker to disclose or withhold the existence of previously received offers

The listing agreements for land, residential and commercial property are usually different.

QUALIFY BUYER

To successfully execute a property sale, a seller must know if the prospective buyer is financially qualified. Entering into a contract with a buyer, who is unqualified, may result in unnecessary and avoidable problems and lead to sheer waste of valuable marketing and sales effort and time. Verifying a potential buyer's financial qualifications is the smart thing to do prior to signing a contract.

Qualifying a buyer is the ability to separate the non-motivated buyers from the motivated ones. A specific series of questions help in qualifying the buyer such as,

1) How long the buyer has been looking out. Longer the time, lower the motivation.

2) Does the buyer need to sell the current home before buying?

3) Has the buyer been pre-qualified by a lender for mortgage?

4) Is the buyer working with another agent?

Qualifying buyers is quite simple. Serious buyers are aware of the stiff competition involved in purchasing a home. Hence they usually acquire a preliminary mortgage approval prior to hunting for properties. Applying for a mortgage pre-qualification letter is an easy process for a property buyer. The mortgage lender verifies the buyer's income, credit and debt, and if found satisfactorily, the buyer is issued a pre-qualification letter. Buyers having a good credit history can obtain such a letter within 24 hours. The mortgage lender also checks if the buyer has adequate money for down payment and meeting closing costs. The mortgage also needs to know the property's selling price and the annual property taxes applicable.

Understanding the financing terms is a vital step in the buyer qualifying process. The pre-qualification letter must indicate the type of loan (FHA, VA, Conventional etc.) applied for and the amount being financed (80%, 90% etc.). During pre-qualification, the buyer must request a good faith closing cost estimate, which helps determine the monthly payout and cash for closing.

In case the seller offers owner financing or holds second mortgage, the buyer must submit a credit report copy (most recent one) to highlight his or her money management capabilities. If the buyer intends to make a cash purchase, then the seller should insist on having the buyer's bank statement for verification of sufficient funds in his or her account. If the buyer is expecting to receive a large settlement as a result of a lawsuit, then the seller's attorney should liaise with the buyer's attorney to finalize the settlement date and verifying funds. Settlement dates could get delayed for months or postponed by a court judge.

Qualifying a buyer is critical for a successful real estate transaction. If the buyer does not possess a pre-qualification letter, then contract signing should be withheld until the buyer acquires one.

SHOWING

Showing the property meant for sale, to the prospective buyer(s) is a significant step of the selling process. The buyers must be greeted in a friendly manner. A brief introduction and offering a property profile sheet is a good way to begin. The buyers may be allowed to look around the property by themselves if they prefer or may be given a guided tour. After the look-around or tour the buyers' queries or questions, if any, have to be answered to their satisfaction. Valuables must be kept in a safe place and basic safety measures must be followed during this phase.

Properties sell themselves. Hence preparing and pricing the property is essential for success. Practicing 'showing' to a friend or neighbor is a good way to prepare for the real event.

Important property information must be placed on a table or countertop to enable the buyer to review. Such property documents may include;

- ➤ A sign-in sheet for the buyer

- ➤ Property profile sheet

- ➤ Property condition disclosure from the seller

- ➤ Home inspection report

- ➤ Property improvement form filled-in by the seller

> ➢ Finance sheets indicating monthly payment and closing cost estimates

> ➢ Tax and utility bills

> ➢ Market analysis or appraisal report

> ➢ Property survey report

> ➢ Photos of the property in different seasons

The property must be cleaned and organized well prior to showing. Prospective buyers will be interested in the property's size, layout, foundation, amenities, taxes, utility budgets, décor, landscaping and neighborhood, besides other features within it. Flexibility is an important characteristic during a showing. Misrepresentation and inaccurate information should be avoided as it could jeopardize the sale and result in expensive litigation.

Buyer tastes and needs may vary vastly; hence buyer's concerns must be addressed carefully. Asking the buyer for a sale, reasonable follow-up and obtaining their feedback are the important next steps. If the buyer makes an offer, review it, negotiate, but be rational and ready to compromise keeping in view the ultimate goal of selling the property

PURCHASE AND SALE AGREEMENT

(M.G.L. c. 84. § 17A) The Purchase and Sale (P&S) Agreement is the contract that governs a transaction between a Buyer and a Seller with respect to the property that is being sold / bought. The P&S is signed after the execution of the initial Offer to Purchase. The P&S is more detailed and contains all the terms and conditions that are mutually agreed between the Buyer and the Seller. It is the final contract agreement that is binding on both parties.

The P&S is a legal document that supersedes the initial offer and is considered as a "long form" contract. The key components of the purchase and sale agreement are;

➢ Names of the Parties

The names and addresses of both, the Buyer and the Seller are stated, in detail, in the purchase and sale agreement, in order to make this document effectively binding on both the parties.

➢ Description of Land

Since a real estate contract requires an accurate description of the property to be transacted (bought and sold), the P&S includes a reference to the record (book and page or the document number) of the existing owner's deed, at the Registry of Deeds.

➢ Price / Consideration

The P&S agreement must include the total purchase price or consideration mutually agreed between the Buyer and the Seller along with other financial components such as the amount paid along with the offer-to-purchase (usually in the range of $500 - $1000), the deposit amount being paid with this P&S agreement (generally about 5%) and the balance amount that will be paid at the time of closing of the deal.

➢ Deposit / Escrow

Both the parties involved in the property transaction must mutually agree about the entity for holding deposit funds and the dispute resolution process. All agreements must be in writing and neither party should sign or make payments until all the terms have been clearly understood. An escrow account is a bank account specifically maintained for the purpose of depositing and holding funds that belong to others. The money has to be retained in the escrow account until the successful completion or termination of the transaction.

> Dates

Important dates regarding the property transaction must be appropriately listed in the P&S agreement. These include the mortgage contingency date, the date of closing and any other dates related to special conditions or important milestones.

> Signatures

The Buyer and the Seller have to sign the purchase and sale agreement document. Signing of the P&S is a proof of acceptance of the terms and conditions stated therein by both the parties and make the agreement legal, binding and enforceable.

FINANCING

Once the purchase and sale agreement signed, financing the transaction gains significance especially if the buyer plans to mortgage the property and obtain a loan from a financing / lending organization. There are various financing options that the buyer can choose from, for purchasing the property, ranging from self-financing, owner financing, lease option and mortgage financing. Some of these are listed and explained below;

> Self- Financing

In this type of financing, the buyer arranges for finance to purchase the property on his or her own, without borrowing from a third party. The buyer may arrange for the required amount through own savings, inheritance, successful lawsuit claims or any other such legitimate means.

> Owner Financing

Owner financing involves a lease agreement between the owner (seller) and the buyer (tenant), where the owner provides the buyer with finance and the buyer pays back in installments. The term of such a loan, interest rates and installments and any other conditions are mutually agreed upon by the seller and the buyer. The buyer pays the amount over the agreed time period and becomes the owner of the property on expiry of such time period as long as all the terms and conditions of their agreement are fulfilled

➤ Lease Option

This type of financing is similar to owner financing with a few differences. In this case too, the owner (seller) and the buyer enter into a lease agreement. The buyer has the option to purchase the property at a pre-agreed price, before expiry of the lease period. However, the buyer may finance the purchase through any third party lender and the owner does not finance the purchase.

➤ Mortgage Loans (M.G.L. c. 167E)

    ○ Fixed-Rate Mortgage

Fixed-rate loans are usually disbursed for repayment terms of 10, 15, 20 or 30 years. The best advantage of this type of financing is that the mortgagee has a clear view of the monthly principal and interest payment, which is usually consistent throughout the term of the loan. Another advantage is that this loan can be re-financed if the interest rates drop significant during the loan term.

But this long-term loan type is the smartest and safest option for property buyers who intend to occupy their property or retain it for at least 10 years or more. If the home buyer is certain of moving out or selling the property in the next five years or less, then an adjustable rate mortgage would be a more suitable option.

    ○ Adjustable-Rate Mortgage (ARM) (M.G.L. c. 167E. § 8)

This type of loan offers an initial lower rate of interest compared to the typical fixed-rate loan. However, such low interest rates are subject to changes after a fixed period. The fixed period may extend from a minimum of 1 year to a maximum of 10 years with options of 3, 5 and 7 years. In this case the interest rate fluctuates in sync with a combination of an indexed rate and a fixed margin with predetermined adjustment intervals. Such adjustments have a minimum and maximum rate ceiling associated with them. ARM loans are popular amongst property buyers planning to occupy it for a long time period or in a booming market with rapidly appreciating prices or planning to refinance in a falling interest rate market.

The initial lower interest rates offered by an ARM may make the buyer eligible for a higher loan amount. After the initial adjustment period, the interest rates usually increase and it is assumed that the buyer will save enough amounts during the adjustment period to account for such increased rates. It is a good practice to calculate and estimate the payment at the ceiling rates (typically up to 6 percent higher than normal) to assess the maximum payment in such a scenario. This will help in preventing payment defaults.

- 1-year Treasury ARM

  In this type of loan, the interest rate remains fixed for the first year and becomes adjustable every subsequent year. The new rate is established on the basis of the treasury average index combined with the loan margin (usually pegged at 2.25 – 2.5 percent). Since the interest rate here is lower than the fixed-rate mortgage, the buyer benefits every time the rates go down. However, it is best to track the margin since it is added to the index to derive the new rate at the expiry of the adjustment period. Contrarily, when the interest rates are rising, the buyer ends up paying more interest than the fixed rate.

- Intermediate ARM

  In case of an intermediate ARM, also known as a hybrid ARM, the interest rate remains constant for a specific time period and then adjusts according to a predetermined schedule. This is indicated by the number of years for which the loan interest is fixed as well as the adjustment intervals. The new rate is derived from an economic index (usually treasury) topped up with the loan margin (2.25 – 2.5 percent). In case of rising interest rates scenario, the buyer ends up paying higher interest as compared to a fixed-rate loan after the end of the initial time period. If the buyer intends to sell off the property in a short term then this is a suitable option as the initial lower interest rates prove beneficial. However, fluctuating interest rates translate into higher payments over the loan tenure.

- Flexible Payment Option (ARM)

  In this type of ARM, the mortgagee can select from a number of payment method options each month. However, there is a restriction on the extent of payment variations in a year. Flexible payment option frees up blocked cash and generates liquid funds at the time of need. This option is good for people with variable incomes such as salespersons working on commission basis.

  Some options don't cover even the interest and hence with lower payments the balance outstanding increases every month, leading to a substantial increase in payments eventually. This could result in negative amortization. Ultimately the mortgagee will have to pay down the principal amount and experience a sharp rise in his or her payments. If the mortgagee is unable to pay, he or she will lose the property. So most financial experts recommend avoiding this option.

- Interest Only ARM

  This type of mortgage works by allowing the mortgagee to pay only the interest amount for a specific period of time and not pay down the principal amount. If the buyer plans to dispose the property in the short term then he or she can purchase real estate that is normally unaffordable. If the real estate or the neighborhood is hot the monthly payments will be low due to the interest-only option while the value of the property appreciates rapidly. The buyer can also choose to pay a higher amount each month, if affordable, to cover the principal. At some point the entire principal will have to be paid down. If the property value dips or the buyer's income falls, then making payment becomes troublesome. If payment of interest and principal together is not possible for the buyer then he or she probably can't afford to purchase the property.

- Convertible ARM

  This type of ARM may be converted into a fixed-rate ARM after a certain time period. In such a convertible loan the fixed-rate is usually higher. The borrower can't seek a more suitable deal later, as in the case of 'refinance'. The advantage that this type of ARM offers is the savings in the loan costs and the avoiding the trouble to shop for loans. But if the refinance rates are lower than the new fixed rates, the borrower will feel the pinch. Experts suggest opting for refinance instead.

➢ Jumbo Loans

In a jumbo loan, the loan amount is higher than the guidelines specified by Freddie Mac and Fannie Mae. In case of a very strong market scenario, jumbo loans increase the possibility of a property purchase, but they involve higher down payments and interest rates.

➢ FHA Loans

Federal Housing Administration (FHA) loan is a government-subsidized loan that includes low down payment (about 3.5 % for takers with qualified credit scores) and closing fees as well. This type of loan is popular amongst first-time home buyers. FHA loans offer lower rates for those who can't afford the down payment or those with not-so-good credit. But, if 10% or more down payment is affordable, then the borrower may find better interest rates with conventional loans. Lenders receive a 2% service fee from the government so the borrower must get a corresponding discount in comparison with similar rate loans.

Borrowers are required to pay an upfront, increased mortgage insurance premium (MIP) equal to 2.25% of the loan amount. The maximum annual MIP is also increased to lower upfront costs. Borrowers with a lower credit score (below 580) are required to down pay a minimum of 10% of the loan amount. Seller credits linked to closing costs are lowered by 50% and restricted to a ceiling of 3% of the property purchase price. Enforcement on FHA-approved lenders will increase continuously and lender performance rankings will be publicly reported to enhance transparency and accountability.

➢ VA Loans

Veteran Administration (VA) loans are zero down payment loans which are offered to veterans only. These loans carry a VA guarantee for the lenders and can be obtained by the borrower with no down payment or mortgage insurance. Further, this loan is assumable. The interest rate for such loans could be possibly higher than conventional or FHA loans so looking around for a good deal is a wise thing to do. The government pays the lenders a 2% service fee, so this should be passed on as a discount to the borrower when compared with a similar rate loan.

> USDA Loans

The Unites States Department of Agriculture (USDA) offers a mortgage loan, which is lesser known, but may be available in Massachusetts and beyond. This loan is an alternative to the popular FHA and traditional Freddie / Fannie mortgage loans. Also known as the Guaranteed Rural Development Housing Section 502 loan, it is meant for persons or households with low to moderate income, for purchasing real estate in a Massachusetts 'rural' community. Borrowers must acquire a proper and complete understanding of the meaning of 'rural' prior to obtaining this loan.

This type of loan offers several vivid benefits to the borrowers such as zero down-payments, nil monthly mortgage insurance, infinite seller contribution, permit to carry out certain repairs on the property and include such repair costs within the total loan amount. This USDA loan requires lower out-of-pocket expenses, lesser guarantee fee and increases flexibility in handling the closing costs related to the transaction. However, for being eligible to buy a home with a rural housing loan, the borrower should be earning a higher income to qualify for a USDA loan as compared to a FHA loan.

> Reverse Mortgage (M.G.L. c. 167E, § 7 and M.G.L. c. 183, § 67)

A reverse mortgage is a type of loan offered to elderly homeowners who need to borrow against their home generally to fund their living expenses. The loan so procured does not have to be repaid until there is a change in ownership of the house. Interest rate is usually set equal to the one year treasury rate with an added margin and an upper limit on the rate change.

The best benefit of this type of mortgage is that it allows persons aged 62 years and above to occupy their homes as they grow older without any repayments. However, the house must be maintained properly, property tax and insurance must be paid regularly. Owners who reverse mortgage their homes are not allowed to obtain a second mortgage, or rent it out or use it for business purposes. These loans being complex in nature, it is important that all the terms and conditions are fully understood to avoid problems later. Selecting a lender with membership of the National Reverse Mortgage Lenders Association is a safe bet.

PASS PAPERS

'Closing' is the final step in the real estate cycle. Closing involves the transfer of ownership of the property from the seller to the buyer. However, this phase involves a lot of documentation work and vital tasks before a successful and satisfactory transfer of ownership of property is executed. The closing process involves the following key steps;

i. Good Faith Estimate (M.G.L. c. 30, § 39M1/2)

Once the mortgage lender and finance type is finalized, the lender is required to provide the buyer with an estimate of all the fees that will be incurred at closing. This document is called the 'Good Faith Estimate' (GFE). It is mandatory for the lender to provide the borrower with the GFE as per the Federal Real Estate Settlement Procedures Act. The lender is supposed to provide the GFE within 3 days of receiving the loan application from the borrower.

Closing fees or settlement costs include nearly every expense related to the property loan. This ranges from 3 percent to 5 percent of the total sale price. The property buyer (loan borrower) should typically commit to the loan only after receiving the good faith estimate from the lender. Ideally, a smart buyer would obtain GFEs from two or more different lenders, compare the closing costs stated in those documents, clarify any large discrepancies and then select the best option.

ii. Opening an Escrow Account (M.G.L. c. 183B, § 43)

An escrow account is an account owned and belonging to a neutral third party, on behalf of the transacting parties (i.e. buyer and the seller). All the money and documents pertaining to the property transaction are held in such an escrow account until all the issues are settled to the complete satisfaction of the seller and buyer. Since the property sale process is an elaborate one, involving several vital steps, opening an escrow account is the best way to protect the interests of both, the buyer and the seller, in any adverse situations.

iii. Conducting a Title Search and Acquiring Title Insurance (M.G.L. c. 185. § 37)

A title search and title insurance provide legal protection and offer peace of mind to the buyer, especially against future claims on the property by a third party such as a spurned relative or a tax collector with unpaid dues. A title office performs a title search to ensure removal of any such third party claims, liens, encumbrances or doubts on the title of the property and confirm its validity. If any problems exist, with respect to the title to the property, then these must be removed prior to transfer of ownership and is usually the responsibility of the seller.

iv. Finding an Attorney

This step is optional, but beneficial, if the buyer wants to obtain professional legal opinion regarding the property documents. Often, even well-educated persons are unable to comprehend or understand the closing documents. An attorney with good experience in the real estate domain can understand the closing documents and scan the right areas for spotting potential problems as well as explain them to the buyer.

v. Understand the Closing Costs

There are numerous costs to be paid at the time of closing and finalization of the property purchase. The HUD-1 statement lists the associated closing costs and this statement must be reviewed and confirmed by and attorney. Some of the standard costs are;

➢ Down payments

➢ Attorney fees

➢ Transaction-related points (e.g. 1 point = 1% of the total loan amount)

➢ Appraisal

➢ Title Search fees

➢ Title Insurance fees

➢ Municipal lien charges

➢ Certified plot plan charges

➢ Credit Score report fees

➢ Insurance Binder (full year)

➢ Recording and Transfer fees

➢ Prepaid interest applicable on the mortgage during the month of closing

➢ Mortgage insurance premium for the first year, unless agreed to be paid on monthly basis

vi. Negotiating the Closing Costs

The escrow service providers charge certain fees; they do not provide their services free of cost. However, such service providers often tend to exploit consumers' ignorance to boost their margins by levying 'junk fees'. Although, there is ambiguity in the definition of junk fees, some of the fees that could come under its ambit are those charged for administration, application and appraisal review, ancillaries, email, processing and settlement. A smart buyer can negotiate to eliminate or reduce such unwanted fees. Sometimes, even legitimate closing services fees may be inflated.

vii. Completing the Home Inspection

A home inspection is not mandatory; however, it would be unwise if a buyer does not conduct one. If the buyer observes some serious problem with the property during inspection, then the buyer may backtrack from the deal or insist on the seller to get the problem fixed or ask the seller for payment to have the problem fixed. For this, the purchase offer must include a home-inspection contingency.

viii. Completing the Pest Inspection

A pest inspection is different from a home inspection as it involves a specialist ensuring the absence or removal of wood-destroying insects such as termites or carpenter ants from the property. A property with termite problem is best avoided as even a small presence can inflate into a destructive and expensive one. Although pests can be removed, the costs involved in eliminating them must be reasonable and borne by or recoverable from the seller prior to the purchase of the property by the buyer. In fact, the mortgage company will insist on fixing even a miniscule pest problem, if found, on the property prior to the closing.

ix. Renegotiating the Offer

Even though the buyer's purchase offer may have been accepted already, if the property inspection reveals any problems, the buyer may renegotiate the purchase price of the property to account for any repair costs likely to be incurred. Or the buyer may let the purchase price remain unchanged, but instead ask the seller to bear the repair costs.

However, if the contract mentions that the property is being purchased 'as is', then the buyer does not have good power to ask for a price reduction or reimbursement of repair costs. But the buyer may still retract from the deal without attracting a penalty, if a major problem is identified and the seller is unable to of refuses to fix it.

x. Locking the Interest Rate

The interest rate offered by a mortgage lender needs to be locked. A good lender tracks the movement of interest rates closely and advises the buyer when rates fall and should be locked. Interest rates are unpredictable and fluctuate many times in a day, so trying to lock-in at the lowest level is not practical. The buyer should be satisfied with a reasonable and affordable rate considering the present market conditions. Interest rates also vary according to the credit score, geographic area and the loan type, so getting the best rates advertised may not be possible.

xi. Eliminating Contingencies

A well-drafted purchase offer usually provisions for several contingencies and is subject to;

➢ The buyer obtaining an interest rate within a certain percentage limit that is affordable.

> ➢ No major problems being revealed with the property during inspection.

> ➢ The seller disclosing all known problems with the property.

> ➢ The pest inspection not uncovering any serious infestation or damage to the property.

> ➢ The seller carrying out necessary repairs as agreed with the buyer.

> ➢ Satisfactory Title V inspection indicating that the private septic system of the property (which does not use the city / town sewerage) conforms to the state and local health board specifications.

> ➢ Satisfactory well water inspection indicating that the private water source of the property provides water quality of acceptable standards.

> ➢ Satisfactory radon test indicating absence of radon

Such contingencies have to be corrected by certain dates (also called 'active approval') and must be included in writing usually within the purchase offer, prior to the transaction being closed. However, some purchase agreements include passive approval of contingencies (also called 'constructive approvals) where the buyer does not object to the seller exceeding the pre-agreed deadlines.

xii. Funding the Escrow Account

At the time of signing the purchase agreement, the buyer is required to deposit some amount as 'earnest money' in the escrow account. This is an indication to the seller that the buyer is 'earnest' about his or her intention to buy the property. This is important because the seller delists the property from the market to enable the buyer to purchase it. If the buyer backs out of the deal the seller forfeits the earnest money as compensation and if the seller backs out of the transaction the buyer is refunded the earnest money.

But prior to closing the transaction, the buyer has to deposit additional amounts into the escrow account. The earnest money deposited is usually adjusted towards the initial down payment. However, the buyer is required to deposit the balance down payment and the closing costs (if to the buyer's account).

xiii. Doing the Final Walkthrough

As a penultimate step, prior to signing the pass papers, the buyer must take one last walk through the property. This is necessary to ensure that no damage has been inflicted in the interim period and items listed in the purchase document are not removed.

xiv. Important 'Closing' Papers

A number of forms have to be reviewed and signed at the time of closing. The buyer's attorney should have reviewed these along with the buyer, well in advance. Some of the key documents to be signed during closing are;

> ➢ HUD-1 Settlement Statement

The HUD-1 settlement statement includes details of the property purchase transaction. This document is divided into two equal halves. The left half lists the details of the borrower and the right one that of the seller.

In this form, the left side lists all the money due from the borrower and refunded to him or her, including money already paid and that which is due to be paid to the lender, attorney, seller and others. The right side lists the loan proceeds (due to the seller from the lender) and the seller's mortgage payoff, if applicable. The taxes and insurance details are also listed here and should be checked by the closing attorney.

> ➢ HUD Addendum

This document lists the break-up and estimates of the escrowed monies that the borrower owes the lender in the form of taxes, hazard and mortgage insurance.

> ➢ Mortgage Note

The mortgage note stands for the buyer's promise to pay the lender in accordance with the terms agreed upon. It is a legal IOU. This Note lists the penalties imposable if the buyer defaults on repayment of the loan and serves as a warning to the buyer about the lenders right to demand full payment ('call the loan) before the loan term ends

.

> Mortgage

The mortgage is the legal agreement that secures the mortgage note and provides the lender a claim against the property if the buyer defaults on the terms agreed in the mortgage note. The mortgage document lists the final scheduled payment date; the borrower's responsibility to pay the principal, interest, taxes and insurance on time; maintain an unbroken hazard insurance and ensure peak condition of the property without deterioration.

Failure to fulfill these requirements by the borrower will empower the lender to demand full payment of the outstanding loan amount. The borrower's default also bestows on the lender the right to foreclose and sell the property and adjust the sale proceeds against the balance loan and foreclosure costs.

> The Final Truth-in-Lending Act (TILA) Statement

The lender has to provide all the loan applicants a Final Truth-in-Lending Act statement within three days from the receipt of the loan application. This statement specifies the Annual Percentage Rate (APR) indicating the mortgage cost as an annual rate. This rate could be greater than the interest rate specified in the mortgage since the APR encompasses all points, fees and credit costs. This statement also describes other loan terms such as amount financed, finance charges and total payment due. If the information changes then the lender is obligated to furnish an updated statement at or prior to closing.

> Lead Paint Indemnification / Disclosure

In this form, the borrower agrees to shield the lender from any harm arising from any incident of lead paint poisoning of a child below the age of 6 years.

➢ Urea Formaldehyde Foam Insulation (UFFI) Indemnification / Disclosure

In this form, the seller confirms the existence or nonexistence of UFFI and agrees to shield the lender from any harm concerning UFFI on the basis of the seller's statement.

➢ Cranston – Gonzales Disclosure

This is an estimate making the borrower aware of the possibility (usually in the form of a percentage) that the lender originating the mortgage loan will service it i.e. collect monthly payments after the loan closure. Servicing is commonly traded as a commodity to other institutions or agents.

➢ Deed

The seller is required to carry the duly signed and notarized deed to the closing. The deed transfers property ownership to the buyer from the seller.

➢ Homestead Declaration

In Massachusetts, by registering a Homestead Declaration, property owners can protect up to $500,000 of the equity in their currently occupied property (residence) against claims from unsecured creditors. Such a declaration has to be filed at the registry of deeds. The closing attorney can file this declaration for a fee and the buyer must inform the closing attorney about his or her desire to do so shortly before the closing. Filing a homestead declaration is an inexpensive way of protecting the property equity.

➢ Affidavits and Disclosures

The state law, lenders or other agencies involved may require the buyer to various affidavits (such as intent to occupy the property) and disclosures (such as administrative details of escrow account during the year). If false information is furnished, the buyer may face criminal penalties or the risk of the lender calling-in the loan.

➤ Title Insurance

The lender may insist on the borrower to buy a lender's insurance policy during the closing for protecting the lender against any liens or title defects (adversely impacting ownership rights) that may arise in the future concerning the property being transacted.

The buyer may also purchase an owner's title insurance policy just prior to the closing to protect his or her ownership interest in the property. This insurance policy is inexpensive and provides coverage during the full ownership tenure. The closing attorney can obtain this policy for the buyer.

➤ Other Lender Forms

The other forms that the lender commonly requires the borrower to sign include the final mortgage application, IRS form W-9, taxpayer certification and identification and the smoke detector certification, flood insurance, rent loss insurance, condominium insurance and other incidental documents.

xv. Signing the Papers

The last and the most vital step of the closing stage is the signing of the pass papers. These may include about a 100 pages or more. The buyer may be under pressure from the notary and the mortgage lender to sign quickly. However, prior to signing, the buyer must read each page thoroughly, especially the fine print which could significantly impact the buyer's finances and life post-purchase.

Particular attention must be focused on ensuring the correct interest rate and the exclusion of any prepayment penalty clause. The buyer must compare the closing costs with the good faith estimate (GFE) received from the lender during the initial stages of the mortgage application. Any fees that exceed 10% of the given estimate must be negotiated by the buyer and reduction obtained.

The closing can be a painfully slow process as the buyer or the seller may have to wait for the other or some third party to take necessary action to proceed forward. It also involves a lot of paperwork. However, patience helps the buyer tide over this phase as long as he or she has done proper research and is confident of ensuring a smooth closing.

FINANCING PROCEDURE

(M.G.L. c. 183. § 17A)

On reading this section completely, you will understand;

- What are the steps involved prior to and while making a mortgage application?
- What are the three key parameters that banks scrutinize prior to approving a loan for purchasing property?
- What is the purchase and sale financing clause?

MORTGAGE APPLICATION

Once the purchase and sale agreement is signed, the next important step for the buyer is the property financing. If the buyer wishes to opt for a loan from a lending institution then the new property will have to be mortgaged. The mortgage process can start even before the signing of the purchase and sale agreement. This includes the following steps;

➢ Shopping for a Loan

An important and time-consuming task related to the home buying process is looking around for the most suitable loan from amongst the plethora of options available. An educated buyer will usually compare the terms of various loan options offered by different lenders and then make a well-informed decision on the best loan option for him or her.

➢ Understanding Mortgage Loans

The mortgage application process can be confusing and filled with uncertainty, especially for first-time home buyers. The buyer could be seeking answers to several questions such as, which is the best type of mortgage; what do lending institutions look for in a mortgage application; and so on. Some of the key factors that new home buyers should compare are;

- The loan interest rate

- Whether a fixed or adjustable interest rate

- Interest rate lock-in while applying for mortgage, time period and costs

- The closing costs

- Additional Fees charged

For acquiring a MassHousing loan, the buyer will have to approach a participating and approved lender. These may vary depending on the loan program suitable for the buyer.

➤ Pre-Qualification / Pre-Approval

Pre-qualification is the process where buyer approaches a lender and submits the necessary documents / information, on the basis of which, the lender determines whether the buyer is qualified for a mortgage loan. Pre-qualification does not guarantee a loan or a specific interest rate at which the lender will offer a loan.

In contrast, a Pre-approval guarantees (usually for a 30 to 45 days period) a mortgage loan at a particular rate. Pre-approval offers the property seller confidence about the ability of the buyer to obtain a mortgage. However, a pre-qualification does provide the buyer an edge over other buyers.

➤ Documentation

The bank or lending institution demands a number of documents as proof of the borrower's assets, income, financial information and credit quality, to be submitted along with the mortgage application. Such documents may include;

- W2 forms pertaining to the previous two years

- Earning statements

- Federal Tax returns

○ Most recent month's paycheck stub displaying the borrower's name and social security number

○ Borrower's year-to-date earnings

○ Proof of name and address of the borrower's employer

○ Proof of other income such as earnings from a second job, commissions / bonuses, overtime, interest and dividends received, VA and retirement benefits, Social Security disbursements, child and alimony support etc.

○ Creditors' list such as credit cards, car and student loans, alimony and child support etc. Proof of minimum monthly payments and account balances of the borrower may also be required.

○ Investment documents such as mutual fund statements, stock certificates, property and automobile licenses and any other investments or assets.

○ Canceled checks indicating mortgage and rental payments.

○ Property sales contract showing the purchase price if a suitable property is already identified.

Keeping the above documents handy before applying for a mortgage loan would help in saving valuable time, although borrowers with a high credit score will not be required to produce all the above documents. Also, not all lenders demand all the above mentioned documents.

BANK APPROVAL STEPS

While evaluating borrowers prior to extending loans, the lending institutions such as banks or non-banking finance companies etc. try to ascertain the borrower's creditworthiness and determine the interest rate to be charged. There are three key parameters that they check to establish the borrower's creditworthiness. These are;

Property

The lenders are interested in calculating the Loan-to-Value Ratio (LTV). This is the ration of the amount of mortgage that the borrower wants and the total worth of the property. This is calculated by simply dividing the mortgage amount with the property price. For example, if property price is $100000 and the mortgage amount applied for is $80000 then the LTV is 80%.

Normally, lending institutions prefer to maintain the loan-to-value ratio at 80% or less, however, some lenders may approve an LTV that is higher than the value of the property. These are known as 'high LTV' loans. Here the interest rates are obviously higher and the borrower must be earning enough in order to be able to pay the monthly payments and become eligible for the loan.

If the borrower already owns a property and is opting for an equity loan, then the lending institution will do an appraisal to estimate the present fair market value (FMV) of the property, since it would have changed from the time it was purchased. The existing mortgage amount is added to the equity loan or credit amount applied for and this is divided by the present value of the property, resulting in a new LTV.

Ability to Pay

One of the most important factors that lenders want to assess is the borrower's ability to pay back the loan every month. For this, they are keen to know how much the borrower is earning, the number of years that the borrower has been working in his or her present job and the number of years of overall experience in a particular field.

Lenders usually calculate the borrower's debt-to-income ratio which includes the part of the monthly income scheduled for existing mortgage payment, if any; car loan payments; credit card bills; and such other obligations as well as the payment towards the new equity debt applied for. Most lenders prefer to maintain this ratio less than or equal to 36%.

Credit Check

Lenders conduct a credit check on the borrower who applies for a mortgage loan. They approach credit bureaus, which collect and maintain a complete record of each individual's existing debt, whether payments are made on time and such other relevant information. This information is compiled into a document called the 'credit report' and it is subjected to a points system to arrive at score ranging between 300 and 850. This is the 'credit score' of the individual or borrower, which is also called as 'FICO score' (named after its pioneer - Fair Isaac Corp.)

Such a credit score can be directly obtained from Fair Isaac or through any other authorized credit bureau. Every person is entitled to obtain one free credit report in a year, as per Federal law. The report and the credit score may be combined or offered separately.

In Massachusetts, the 'standard' form purchase and sale agreement includes a mortgage contingency clause which extends protection to the property buyer and his or her deposit for a certain time period until he or she acquires a firm loan commitment. The cut-off date is negotiated and mutually agreed between the buyer and seller and is generally fixed at about 30 days from the signing of the purchase and sale agreement. If the buyer fails to obtain a firm loan commitment from a lender prior to the deadline, he or she can back out of the agreement and claim full refund of the deposit.

In such situations, the buyer may opt for one of the two choices; either seek an extension of the deadline from the seller or terminate the agreement.

In other words, the mortgage contingency clause or loan contingency clause is a provision in the purchase and sale agreement stating that the if the prospective buyer fails to get a mortgage within a certain time period and on the specified terms then he or she may terminate the entire deal and claim back the deposit. Hence the buyer's agreement with the seller is conditional upon him or her successfully obtaining a mortgage on the property.

The mortgage contingency clause in the 'standard' form purchase and sale agreement is usually negotiable between the buyer and the seller. The seller would desire to close the sale irrespective of the interest rates being very high or the mortgage terms being highly unsuitable for the buyer. On the other hand, the buyer would want to ensure that if he or she does not obtain the desired terms such as 90% financing, 30-year loan term and Z% interest rate, then the transaction can be terminated and the down payment recovered from the seller. The seller may find such conditions very uncertain and unfair. Therefore, the buyer and the seller have to often compromise on the financing clause provisions.

TYPES OF LENDING INSTITUTIONS

On reading this section completely, you will understand;

- What are the different types of finance / loan lending institutions?
- What is Federal Savings & Loan?
- What are commercial banks and their functions?
- What are mutual savings banks and their business?
- What are cooperative banks and their role in mortgage financing?
- What are credit unions and their area of operations?
- What role do mortgage companies play in mortgage financing?
- How are life insurance companies involved with property mortgages?
- What are the benefits of obtaining loans from private lenders?

FEDERAL SAVINGS AND LOAN

A savings and loan association (S&L), also called 'thrift', is a state or federally chartered financial institution that focuses on accepting savings deposits from individuals and issuing long-term mortgage loans as well as other loans. Their main purpose is to issue mortgage loan against residential property, primarily addressing single-family residences. S&L associations are mutually held and privately managed, where the depositors and borrowers get membership and voting rights and the power to set financial and managerial goals of the association. S&L associations can also be joint-stock companies or publicly traded, but in such cases, the depositors and borrowers are not possess membership rights and managerial control.

In 1932, the Federal Home Loan Bank Act was passed and the Federal Home Loan Bank was formed to assist banks in offering long term, amortized loans for purchasing homes. The intent was to transfer the property purchase funding function from insurance companies (which were the prime lending institutions until then) to banks. S&L associations then started providing low-cost funding through the Federal Home Loan Bank for mortgage lending. The law restricts the lending by thrifts to a maximum of 20 percent in commercial loans due to their vulnerability to housing downturns.

COMMERCIAL BANKS

Commercial banks are financial institutions that offer a wide variety of services such as accepting deposits, issuing business loans and providing basic investment products. Such banks usually deal with corporations or large businesses instead of general public individuals or small business.

One of their key lending businesses, among numerous other services, is the issuance of mortgage loans. These loans are a common debt instrument, used for the purpose of buying real estate. The bank gets a lien on the title to the property as security for extending the loan, until the loan is fully paid off. In case of a default by the borrower in repaying the loan, the bank can exercise its right to repossess the property and sell it to recover the money owed to it.

Traditionally, commercial banks have invested only a small percentage of their total assets in extending mortgage loans. However, recent changes in banking laws and policies have shifted their focus back to mortgages.

MUTUAL SAVINGS BANKS

This type of financial institution is chartered by a regional or central government, without any capital shares owned by its members contributing to a universal fund. These members own this business. All claims, loans etc. are issued from this fund and profits after necessary deductions are shared among the members. Such banks serve as a safe repository for individual members to deposit and invest their savings in stocks, bonds, mortgages, loans and other securities and share the resulting profits or losses proportionately.

Mutual Savings Banks were formed to encourage savings by individuals. Their prime function is to protect deposits, invest securely within limits and offer interest to depositors. Unlike commercial banks, such banks don't have any stockholders. All the profit generated, after reducing the operating costs, belongs to the depositors. These banks emphasize security and hence conservative in their investment. This conservative approach makes them stable and reliable entities.

COOPERATIVE BANKS

(M.G.L. c. 183. § 22) Cooperative banks are engaged in the business of retail and commercial banking structured on a cooperative format. Such institutions accept deposits and lend money. Their retail and commercial banking services are similar to those offered to cooperative businesses by other financial institutions such as mutual savings banks and credit unions etc.

Such banks are owned by their clients and tread the path of cooperative principles (i.e. one person, one vote). They accept deposits and extend loans to non-members too, besides regular members, and hence are partly owned by non-members. Some cooperative banks are publicly traded on stock exchanges, diluting the stake of their members and making them semi-cooperative.

(M.G.L. c. 171. § 65A)

Credit unions are member-owned financial institutions that are democratically governed by their members. These are formed and operated with the objectives of promoting thrift, providing loans at reasonable rates and offering other financial services to all its members. Credit Unions are community oriented, not profits oriented and serve people. These unions are funded wholly by member deposits and avoid external borrowings. All individuals having accounts in credit unions have membership and ownership rights. Credit unions are similar and smaller forms of cooperative banks. These are usually strictly governed by the guidelines established by the World Council of Credit Unions (WOCCU).

Credit unions are required to generate sufficient revenue to cover their operating expenses; else they may shutdown like any other business. Credit union rules on responsible lending limit their lending to small amounts and to fewer people, despite such people having repaying capability, thus increasing their risk of failure.

(M.G.L. c. 255E, § 2)

Mortgage companies are those that offer loan against securities such as a home or car etc. Apart from banks and housing finance companies, non-banking financial institutions also offer mortgage loans on similar terms as regular finance companies. They could be self-financed or source their finance from a larger financial institution or bank or offer packages from such companies for a fee or higher interest rate.

Mortgage brokers are intermediary companies who broker mortgage loans for individuals or businesses. They search and identify banks or private lenders offering specific loans that a borrower is seeking. Such brokers charge the lenders and not borrowers with good credit applications. They are usually governed by local jurisdictions to ensure compliance with banking and finance laws.

A 'Mortgage Bank' engages in the business of originating and / or servicing loans against securities. It is a state-licensed banking body that offers loans to consumers directly. They fund loans with self-financed capital and do not accept deposits from individuals or businesses. Mortgage banks originate loans, place them on pre-set warehouse line of credit until sold to investors like Fannie Mae or Freddie Mac. This is called a secondary market transaction. Their two primary sources of income are loan origination fees and servicing fees (if they service loans).

LIFE INSURANCE COMPANIES

Insurance is a fair transfer of risk due to loss, from one individual / body to another, in return for a certain fee. Life insurance companies are insurers or assurers who offer policies (contracts) to individuals (the insured or policy holders), to cover (pay lump sum amount of money) their life in case of any adverse incident such as death or permanent disability due to accident etc. in return for a premium (money paid in lump sum or regular instalments). There are various types of life insurance policies meant for the purpose of protection or investment or both.

A person obtaining a mortgage loan against property usually has to buy a life insurance policy to cover the loan repayment obligation in case of his / her death or loss of income or permanent disability due to accident etc. prior to complete repayment of the loan. This is where life insurance policies play an important role in the property purchase transaction.

PRIVATE LENDERS

(M.G.L. c. 255E, § 2)

Private lenders (or creditors) are persons, firms or organizations which offer loans or financial services to a second party (person or institution), called debtors / borrowers, enforced by a contract and in expectation of some financial returns.

Private lenders could be wealthy individuals with high net worth; trusts representing individuals; umbrella firms formed by a group of two or more persons pooling funds together; real estate investment trusts and other general investment trusts.

Such private lenders offer loans to interested borrowers on similar terms as banks and other financial institutions. They could be more flexible with less stringent rules than the formal entities but their loans or products may come with higher interest rates.

On reading this section completely, you will understand;

- What is a Discount rate?
- What does Prime rate mean?
- What are mortgage rates?
- What is the meaning of Discounts or Points with respect to mortgage financing?
- How are buy downs beneficial as a mortgage financing method?

RELATIONSHIP BETWEEN DISCOUNT RATE, PRIME RATE, MORTGAGE RATES

Discount Rate

Many lenders offer loans that come with a slightly lower than regular interest rate for a fixed initial time period, usually ranging from one to three years, to attract prospective borrowers. This is called a 'Discount Rate'.

For example, most lenders offer loans with an annual percentage rate (APR) that is 'discounted'. It is not linked to the index rate (prime rate) which is used for subsequent rate adjustments. Such a discounted rate is usually offered for a period ranging between 12 months to 36 months, after which the standard index-linked rate becomes applicable.

Prime Rate

Prime rate or prime lending rate is the term used to refer to the interest rates levied by most banks. Prime rate originally meant the benchmark interest rate at which banks offered loans to favored customers i.e. those having a good credit history, though this is no more relevant. The central bank determines the prime rate and most banks are quick to adjust their lending rates accordingly. Today, certain interest rates are conveyed as percentage points above or below the prime rate.

The prime rate is commonly used as an index for calculating rate changes in adjustable rate mortgages (ARM) and other short-term variable rate loans.

Various home equity lines of credit (HELOC) and credit cards charging variable interest rates mention them as the prime rate plus a certain fixed value often known as the 'spread' or 'margin'.

Mortgage Rates

Mortgage rates are the interest rates that lenders charge when extending loans against securities (mortgages) such as title to a property or other significant assets, to borrowers. In short, it is a financial charge that a lender levies for allowing the use of their money. Mortgage interest rates are of various types such as 'fixed rate' or 'adjustable rate' (also called 'variable rate' or 'floating rate'), VA rates and FHA rates etc. as explained in Section 1 of this Chapter.

Often, mortgage rates are negotiable and depend on the credentials of the borrower or specific conditions. These rates are usually linked to (above, below or equal) the prime rate and commonly expressed as a percentage of the prime rate.

DISCOUNTS OR POINTS

Points, also called 'discount points', are a type of pre-paid interest. One point is equivalent to one percent of the mortgage loan amount. By charging points to the borrower, the lender practically enhances the yield on the disbursed loan, beyond the applicable interest rate. On the other hand, borrowers may pay a lender points as a means of reducing the interest rate applicable on the loan, consequently lowering the monthly payment in lieu of this up-front payment. For every point bought, the loan rate is usually lowered by 1/8% (0.125%).

The buyer will incur a net financial loss if the property is sold or refinanced before reaching the break-even point. The buyer will gain net financial savings if the loan is maintained beyond the break-even point. The longer the property remains financed through the loan availed with the purchase points, the larger will be the pay off from the money spent to purchase the points. If the buyer intends to sell or refinance the property in the short term, then purchasing points will prove costlier than repaying the loan at a higher rate of interest.

The buyer may purchase points to lower the monthly payment in order to qualify for a loan. Qualifying for a loan based on lower monthly payments as compared to monthly income may be possible by lowering the monthly payment through purchasing points to buy down the loan interest rate.

Discount points differ from origination or broker fees. Discount points are always used for interest rate buy down, whereas origination fee may be lender charges for a loan or just another name for interest rate buy down. Both these are included under lender charges in a HUD-1 settlement statement. The savings made over the loan tenure by lowering interest rates using discount points proves beneficial for the buyer and should be opted for if the buyer intends to occupy the home over a long time period.

BUYDOWNS

A buydown is a mortgage financing method in which the buyer tries to negotiate a lower interest rate applicable for at least the initial few years of the mortgage. The property seller generally makes payments to the loan lending institution resulting in it lowering the buyer's monthly interest rate and hence monthly payment. This continues for a period ranging between one to five years.

In a seller's market, the property seller may hike the purchase price to compensate for the buydown costs, however, in most markets the buyer will not benefit from using a buydown as an attraction / lure if the seller intends to raise the price and offset the benefit to the buyer.

In many cases, the buydown involves only the lender and the buyer and excludes the seller. The buydown option can be used for refinancing.

TYPES OF MORTGAGES

On reading this section completely, you will understand;

- What are the different types of mortgages and how are they beneficial to the property buyer?
- What is a conventional mortgage?
- What is a Veterans Administration (VA) mortgage?
- What is a FHA loan and its key features?
- What is MGIC and the type of loan that it offers?
- How does a 'direct reduction' type of mortgage work?
- What is a 'construction' loan and where is it useful?
- What is a blanket mortgage and its characteristics?
- What is a 'package' loan and its use?
- How does a 'demand/open' loan work?
- Why is 'purchase money' mortgaging a good option?
- What is a 'junior / second' mortgage?
- What is the meaning of 'open end' mortgage?
- What are 'wraparound' mortgages?
- How does a 'variable rate' mortgage help in buying a property?
- How does 'balloon mortgage' benefit a property buyer?
- How and with whom is a 'shared equity' mortgage shared?
- What are the consequences of 'negative amortization'?
- What are 'equity loans'?

CONVENTIONAL

Conventional mortgages are simply loans offered by private lenders. These may come with interest rates that are fixed, adjustable, hybrid or other types. Conventional loans have stricter qualifying requirements than government loans, however, they usually involve less paperwork and do not have a cap or ceiling on the loan amount sought.

V. A.

Veteran Administration (VA) loans are zero down payment loans which are offered to veterans only. These loans carry a VA guarantee for the lenders and can be obtained by the borrower with no down payment or mortgage insurance. Further, this loan is assumable. The interest rate for such loans could be possibly higher than conventional or FHA loans so looking around for a good deal is a wise thing to do. The government pays the lenders a 2% service fee, so this should be passed on as a discount to the borrower when compared with a similar rate loan.

F.H.A.

Federal Housing Administration (FHA) loan is a government-subsidized loan that includes low down payment (about 3.5 % for takers with qualified credit scores) and closing fees as well. This type of loan is popular amongst first-time home buyers. FHA loans offer lower rates for those who can't afford the down payment or those with not-so-good credit. But, if 10% or more down payment is affordable, then the borrower may find better interest rates with conventional loans. Lenders receive a 2% service fee from the government so the borrower must get a corresponding discount in comparison with similar rate loans.

Borrowers are required to pay an upfront, increased mortgage insurance premium (MIP) equal to 2.25% of the loan amount. The maximum annual MIP is also increased to lower upfront costs. Borrowers with a lower credit score (below 580) are required to down pay a minimum of 10% of the loan amount. Seller credits linked to closing costs are lowered by 50% and restricted to a ceiling of 3% of the property purchase price. Enforcement on FHA-approved lenders will increase continuously and lender performance rankings will be publicly reported to enhance transparency and accountability.

M.G.I.C.

Mortgage Guarantee Insurance Corporation (MGIC), a group company of MGIC Investment Corporation, provides private mortgage insurance. In addition, it offers lenders a variety of underwriting and allied services and products linked to home mortgage lending.

Founded in 1957 by a real estate attorney, Max H. Karl, its purpose was to insure the top portion of a mortgage instead of the whole of it, for clients who found it difficult to obtain government-backed financing.

Mortgage insurance or mortgage guarantee or home-loan insurance is a policy that covers both lenders and investors from losses that might be incurred on account of default in repaying mortgage loans. Whether mortgage insurance is public or private depends on the insurer.

Private mortgage insurance is necessary in cases where the down payments are lower than 20 percent. Interest rates may vary between 0.32 percent and 1.20 percent of the loan principal per year depending on factors such as percentage of loan insured, credit score, loan-to-value (LTV) ratio and fixed or variable interest rates. The interest can be paid in a single lump sum or annual or monthly installments or a particular combination. Private mortgage insurance can be borrower-paid or lender-paid and the terms and conditions vary accordingly.

DIRECT REDUCTION

Direct reduction mortgage is one where the borrower has to make equal payments of fixed amount during each repayment period (say monthly) agreed upon. Such payments include both, the principal (loan recapture) and interest. A major part of this equal installment amount is apportioned towards the interest and lower part towards the principal, thus declining the principal balance proportionately. The installment portion credited towards the principal increases steadily and that credited towards the interest decreases steadily. At some stage during the loan repayment term, the situation reverses, where a higher amount from the equated installment is credited towards the principal and lower amount is credited towards the interest. By the end of the loan term the principal loan amount is repaid in full by the borrower and the interest rate agreed upon is fully recovered by the lender. The owner's equity in the home increases slowly during the initial period and faster as the end of the loan term nears.

For example, at the start of the mortgage loan, the following scenario is possible;

Principal Amount: $250,000.

Repayment Term: 30 years

Interest Rate: 8%

Monthly Payment: $1700 (including principal and interest components)

In this case, the monthly payment amount remains the same throughout the loan term. The principal component is lower and interest component is higher initially but this ratio reverses somewhere midway.

CONSTRUCTION

A construction mortgage is a private loan that a commercial investor can use to acquire an investment property that he or she intends to hold until the construction is completed and the property is ready for sale. It is usually disbursed in increments linked to the progress of the construction work as the need for funds arises for the borrower to complete the construction. On completion of construction and sale of the property for a profit, the loan extended by the private lender is repaid in full or gradually, as the lender partially releases the collateral given at the time of application. The maximum loan-to-value (LTV) permitted on a subject property equals 70 percent and the disbursements are made to the borrower in accordance with the terms and conditions agreed by both parties in the construction holdback contract signed at closing.

BLANKET

A blanket mortgage is a loan that is allowed to be used to buy more than one property. The multiple properties form the collateral against the blanket mortgage, but such properties are permitted to be sold individually. Most real estate developers leverage blanket mortgage to consolidate the total borrowing that they require for purchasing properties for their real estate business. The blanket mortgage helps the real estate developers to not only pay the cost of the properties but also cover the property development expenses. A blanket mortgage is sometimes used to finance development projects such as cooperatives or proposed subdivisions.

In other words, the blanket loan is secured by multiple properties. Its most important feature is 'release clause' allowing the borrower to sell of a part of the securing properties without refinancing. In traditional mortgages, the borrower is required to pay off the entire loan before selling the securing property.

Residential project developers often use blanket loans to buy large land tracts. The loan is secured during funding by 100% of the land bought. Over a period of time, the developers subdivide the entire property and sell off the smaller pieces individually. When each small piece of land is sold, the security portion corresponding to it is released and the developer pays down the loan partially.

Individual buyers may find it difficult to purchase multiple properties at the same time, unless they have ample income or signed lease agreements to support the repayment. However, individual buyers are often found to leverage blanket loans to simplify transition from selling their existing home to purchasing or constructing the new one. The best benefits of a blanket mortgage are its flexibility and efficiency. It enables an individual to have only one mortgage instead of multiple, to avoid short-term loans that are expensive and to prevent the situation of selling the existing property early and staying in a rental one as a tenant.

In case of a default, the lending institution can take possession of all the properties that secure the blanket loan.

PACKAGE

A package mortgage is a type of real estate loan that is used to fund the purchase of both, real and personal property. For example, a package loan may be used to finance the purchase of a new home including the furnishing such as carpeting, window coverings as well as major appliances.

DEMAND/OPEN

Demand / Open mortgages are usually short-term loans. These loans significantly differ from the standard loans since their repayment schedule does not include fixed payment dates and they come with a floating interest rate which varies in accordance with the prime lending rate (a benchmark / reference interest rate used by banks for offering loans). Demand loans may be 'called' by the lender for repayment at any point in time. Such loans may be secured or unsecured.

PURCHASE MONEY

Purchase-money mortgage is a mortgage extended to the buyer by the property seller to finance the purchase of the property. Such a need arises when the buyer is unable to qualify and obtain a mortgage through the regular lending channels. This is also called owner or seller financing.

A property seller may offer a purchase-money mortgage as an incentive and motivation to the buyer to purchase the property. This is particularly useful in scenarios where the buyer assumes the seller's mortgage and the difference between the sales price and the assumed mortgage is addressed through seller financing.

JUNIOR/SECOND

Residential as well as commercial property owners often obtain more than one mortgage against their property. A borrower may already have a home equity loan and acquire a 'second mortgage' to meet expenses such as home repairs, education funds, medical fees or credit card debts.

Second mortgages, also called 'junior mortgages', include popular loan offerings like home equity lines of credit (HELOC). Such mortgages are often availed by borrowers to leverage the equity in their property for paying other expenses stated above.

A first mortgage, commonly referred to as 'mortgage', is used to purchase the property originally, by signing the mortgage note and the mortgage agreement.

Although, both, first and second mortgage lenders possess foreclosure rights in case of payment default by the borrower, first mortgage lenders have priority over second mortgage holders in recovering payments. In case of a foreclosure sale, the first mortgage is paid off first along with other specific liens or claims, if any, against the property. If sufficient balance is still available, the second mortgage and other creditors are paid off. Second mortgage lenders often recover little, if anything, of their loan outstanding from a foreclosure.

For second mortgage holders, recovery of loan amounts may depend on various factors such as;

> Repayment to first mortgage holders.

> Other liens with higher priority such as tax liens.

> Foreclosure fees and charges due to the priority lenders.

> The recording dates and loan amounts of other secondary loans which determines priority of pay offs against foreclosure proceeds.

> Proper recording of the loan (also called 'perfected' loan) through appropriate documents and in the public records.

A second mortgage generally gets canceled or extinguished in case of foreclosures. However, the borrower still owes the money to such second / junior lenders, who may resort to other options for recovery such as;

> Obtain a deficiency judgment from a court of law against the borrower if the foreclosure sale proceeds are insufficient to compensate the secondary loan.

> Purchase the property during the foreclosure sale.

> Repay the first mortgage prior to the foreclosure sale, gaining priority over the property during the foreclosure sale.

> Challenge in the court, the priority accorded to other liens and loans. This may not be successful as almost all lenders follow procedural norms to protect their lending.

> Initiate the foreclosure proceedings; however, liens and claims with higher priority are paid off first.

No lender likes to lose money; hence second / junior loan lenders should make every possible effort to recover payments due to them.

OPEN END

(M.G.L. c. 183. § 288)

Open-End Mortgage is a type of mortgage that allows the borrower to hike up the mortgage amount when required at a later date. Such mortgages allow the borrower to revert to the lender to obtain more funds if specific conditions are met. Such an additional amount that the lender offers, usually has a pre-set dollar limit.

Open-ended loans allow the borrower to make payments or cash withdrawals within the credit limit specified which, if exceeded, attracts a penalty. Such loans are flexible and provide the borrower with multiple options. In an open-ended line of credit, a borrower pays an interest only if there is an outstanding balance when the payment becomes due.

For example, a borrower acquires $300,000 to buy a home. He gets approval for an open-end mortgage that enables him or her to borrow an additional amount at a later date during the tenure of the loan. However, the condition would be that the total principal amount should not exceed a certain limit, say 80% of the assessed value of the home. This mortgage is similar to HELOC, which enables homeowners to extract equity from their homes. Another example of open-ended credit is a credit card.

WRAPAROUND

Wraparound mortgage, also called 'wrap', is a type of secondary financing availed for purchasing real estate. Here, the seller offers the buyer a junior mortgage that wraps around and co-exists with any original mortgage which has been secured by the property already. In case of a wrap, the seller receives from the buyer a secured promissory note for the amount outstanding on the underlying mortgage and an amount equal to the purchase money balance.

In a wraparound transaction, the lender assumes responsibility of the existing mortgage. For example, person A having a $50000 mortgage on his or her home, sells it to B for $90000. B makes a down payment of $10000 and borrows $80000 through a new mortgage. This new mortgage 'wraps around' the original mortgage of $50000, since the new lender now issues payments on the original mortgage.

The new buyer pays monthly instalments to the seller, who in turn pays the original / superior mortgage lender. If the new buyer defaults on the monthly payments, the seller can foreclose the wraparound mortgage and take possession of the property. Wraps are a type of seller financing that, in effect, reduce the barriers to property ownership and accelerate the process of buying a property.

For example, a seller having an original mortgage sells his or her home along with the first mortgage and creates a second mortgage received from the buyer. This second mortgage equals the first mortgage amount and an additional negotiated amount that is less than or equal to the sales price as well as deduction of down payment and closing costs, if any. The buyer makes monthly payments to the seller, who then repays the first mortgage with the payment received. On sale or refinance of the property by the buyer, all the mortgages are fully repaid and the seller is entitled to the difference amount from the wrap and underlying loan payoffs.

The seller usually charges a 'spread', which is the difference between the seller's first mortgage, say at 6%, and the wraparound mortgage, say at 8%. Thus the seller earns 2% spread on each monthly payment. The actual difference between the principal amounts and the amortization schedules determines the spread earned.

In the above discussed example, assume that the $50000 mortgage has an interest rate of 6% and the new mortgage of $80000 has an interest rate of 8%. The cash outlay of the lender is $30000 ($80000 - $50000) earning him or her 8% interest. In addition, the lender earns 2% (8% - 6%) on $50000.

Since the property title actually transfers from the seller to the buyer in a wrap transaction, such transactions violate the 'due-on-sale' clause, if present, in the underlying mortgage.

The advantage of opting for a wraparound mortgage for selling property is that it usually sells much 'faster' and at a 'premium price' since it includes financing. The disadvantage of a wraparound mortgage is that the seller does not gain any equity (tradeoff for selling faster) or gains some equity as 'monthly payments' but not 'cash at closing' (used for paying closing costs and charges). Further, the seller stays bound to the underlying loan which is wrapped for the buyer.

VARIABLE RATE

Variable rate mortgages, also known as adjustable rate mortgage (ARM) loans offer an initial lower rate of interest compared to the typical fixed-rate loan. However, such low interest rates are subject to changes after a fixed period. The fixed period may extend from a minimum of 1 year to a maximum of 10 years with options of 3, 5 and 7 years. In this case the interest rate fluctuates in sync with a combination of an indexed rate and a fixed margin with predetermined adjustment intervals. Such adjustments have a minimum and maximum rate ceiling associated with them. ARM loans are popular amongst property buyers planning to occupy it for a long time period or in a booming market with rapidly appreciating prices or planning to refinance in a falling interest rate market.

The initial lower interest rates offered by an ARM may make the buyer eligible for a higher loan amount. After the initial adjustment period, the interest rates usually increase and it is assumed that the buyer will save enough amounts during the adjustment period to account for such increased rates. It is a good practice to calculate and estimate the payment at the ceiling rates (typically up to 6 percent higher than normal) to assess the maximum payment in such a scenario. This will help in preventing payment defaults.

BALLOON

In this type of mortgage, the loan is not fully amortized during the entire term of the mortgage note, creating residual dues at maturity. The final installment is known as the 'balloon payment' due to its relatively large size. A balloon mortgage may carry a fixed or floating interest rate and are more common in commercial real estate transactions than residential ones.

A good example of a balloon payment is the Fannie Mae 7-year balloon, which includes monthly payments on a 30-year amortization. The balloon payment amount is required to be mentioned in the contract, if the Truth-in-Lending regulations are application to the loan.

If the borrower is unable to pay the final balloon installment, then the mortgage note may be reset at the then existing market rates and with a full amortizing plan. However, this may be possible only if the borrower owns / occupies the property at that time, has no record of late monthly payments during the previous 12 months and the property is lien-free. Alternatively, the borrower may arrange to refinance (with the associated risk) the property or sell it off to pay the final balloon installment.

SHARED EQUITY

In a shared equity mortgage, the lender offers the buyer a loan (lump sum or regular income) against a share in the equity of the house i.e. a share in the future increase in the value of the house. The borrower has the right to occupy the house (property) until death. The lender has to be repaid at a later date. Older the age of the borrower, smaller is the share that the lender requires.

Also called 'equity release' mortgage, the shared equity mortgage requires the property to be mortgage-free and fully owned by the borrower. This type of loan is beneficial for the elderly and is sometimes referred to as 'reverse mortgage'.

The advantages of a shared equity mortgage are;

> Borrower gets a capital sum of tax-free cash or regular income (annuity), which may be index-linked, until death.

> The amount of inheritance tax applicable on the property is reduced.

> The borrower is protected by the no-negative-equity-guarantee (NNEG) if the housing market experiences a downturn.

> In a scenario of falling interest rates, the borrower may refinance the mortgage with other lenders, at lower rates.

The disadvantages of a shared equity mortgage are;

> The borrower's heirs will inherit lesser amount of money on his or her death, especially if the mortgage interest rate outpaces the growth of the property value.

> A lower amount may be available for bequeathing to charity.

> This is a far more expensive option than disposing the property through a sale, for releasing equity.

NEGATIVE AMORTIZATION

Negative amortization is a situation where the principal balance on a loan increases due the installment payments being lower than the required installment amount, typically because the interest due is not included in it. This is not a default situation since lower installment payments are allowed contractually and the deficit interest amount is added to the loan's principal. This results in an increased principal balance which the borrower owes to the lender.

For example, the interest payment in a regular loan installment may be $500 and the borrower may be paying $400 as agreed with the lender in the contract. The deficit of $100 interest with every installment repayment gets added to the principal balance, thus inflating it over a period of time.

ARMs with negative amortization conditions are called Payment Option ARMs while fixed-rate mortgages with similar conditions are called Graduated Payment mortgages.

Although such low monthly payment mortgages convenience borrowers in the short term, the monthly payments should be increased significantly at some stage of the mortgage term to cover up the deficit. In case of graduated payment mortgages, the date(s) of payment increase are clearly established and certain. However, although payment option ARMs have similar payment increase schedules, specific triggers could result in adverse impact to the mortgage, prior to the scheduled payment increase, thus enhancing the payment shock risk substantially.

EQUITY LOANS

An equity loan is a specific type of mortgage loan, where the borrower receives money from the lender against the property. However, in this case the property is already owned outright by the borrower and not being bought using the loan proceeds. The equity loan provided by the lender is secured by the property.

For example, if a person owns a home valued at $100000 and it is mortgage-free, then the person may obtain an equity loan up to 80% LTV (loan-to-value), which translates to $80000 in cash, by mortgaging the title to his or her home. Many lending institutions allow the borrower to repay just the interest charged on the loan every month. Such interest is calculated on a daily basis and compounded to the loan only once every month. The borrower may use any surplus funds to partly prepay the outstanding loan principal anytime during the loan tenure. The interest calculated gets reduced proportionately from the date of such prepayment. Some mortgage products permit the borrower to redraw cash, if required, up to the original LTV, thus extending the loan term beyond the original determined period.

The interest rate applicable on equity loans is comparatively much lower than on unsecured loans like credit cards, since equity loans are offered against collateral and credit card debt does not involve any collateral.

ASSUME VS "SUBJECT TO"

On reading this section completely, you will understand;

- What is an assumed / assumable mortgage or loan?
- What is a 'subject to' mortgage and when should a buyer opt for it?

Assumed / Assumable Mortgage

An 'assumable' mortgage is that in which an existing borrower can convey or transfer the terms (or obligations) and balance of the existing mortgage to other interested home buyers who are qualified under the lender / guarantor guidelines. Presently, only FHA, VA and USDA mortgage loans are assumable without the lender's permission.

Other fixed-rate mortgage loans usually include a 'due-on-sale' clause that requires the mortgage to be fully repaid in case the property is sold. A due-on-sale clause forbids a home buyer from assuming a seller's existing loan without the lender's consent. If such consent is granted, the interest rate applicable is always equal to the current market rate. Lenders usually include this clause to prevent loan assumptions without their consent and protect their own interests.

For example, a homeowner may be carrying a mortgage of $250000 repayable over a 30-year loan term against his or her residential property. A prospective buyer may be interested in purchasing this property for $300000 and retain the existing mortgage in order to avoid the hassles and costs of applying for a new loan. The buyer may make a down payment of $50000 towards the home equity (differential cost) and officially assume the existing loan, thus taking on liability for the debt.

On completing the assumption of a mortgage loan with the permission of the lender, the seller may ask the lender to provide a release of liability letter. If such an assumption occurs without the lender's permission, the seller is still liable for the debt if the buyer defaults. In case of VA loans, the seller can request a release of liability after the assumption even if the lender's permission was not taken prior to the assumption.

'Subject To' Mortgage

'Subject to' mortgage means buying a property subject to an existing mortgage. In this case, the seller does not pay off the existing mortgage but the buyer (borrower) takes over the payment. The unpaid amount of the existing loan is included in calculating the buyer's purchase price for the property.

The key motivation for a property buyer to purchase a 'subject to' property is taking over the seller's existing mortgage, which usually carries a lower rate of interest. For example, if the current interest rate is 8% and the seller's existing mortgage is having a 6% fixed-interest rate, then the buyer benefits from the 2% difference which could translate to a significant difference in the monthly payment. Another motivation for buying a 'subject to' property is that the buyer may have a bad credit score and does not qualify for a 'subject to' financing, but if the seller is willing to pull the buyer's credit report then the buyer can still buy the 'subject to' home.

'Subject to' loans are usually of three types as explained below;

➢ A straight subject to involving cash-to-loan – Here, the buyer pays cash to the seller for the difference amount between his or her purchase price and the seller's existing loan outstanding. For example, if the existing loan outstanding is $100000 and the sale price is $140000; the buyer pays $40000 in cash to the seller.

➢ A straight subject to involving seller carryback – Seller Carryback (or seller financing) is commonly found as a second mortgage or a land contract or a lease option instrument. For example, if the existing loan outstanding is $100000, new sale price is $150000 and the buyer down pays $20000, then the seller can lend the balance $30000 to the buyer and charge a separate interest rate on it along with other terms negotiated and agreed upon mutually. The buyer makes two payments – one to the seller's lender and another to the seller at a different interest rate.

➢ A wraparound 'subject to' – this allows the seller an override of interest since the seller earns profit on the existing mortgage outstanding. For example, suppose the existing mortgage outstanding is $100000 at an interest rate of 4%, the new sale price is $150000 and the buyer pays down $20000. The seller finances $130000 ($150000 - $20000) to the buyer at an interest rate of say 5%. In this scenario, the seller earns 1% (5% - 4%) on the existing mortgage outstanding of $100000 and 5% on the difference amount of

Difference Between 'subject to' and 'assumed' Mortgage

In case of the 'subject to' deal, both the buyer and the seller do not inform the lender about the property sale transaction and hide the fact that the buyer is now making payments on behalf of the seller, because the buyer would not have taken the lender's consent to take over the mortgage. To protect themselves from such situations, lenders include special verbiage in their mortgage deeds that empower them to call the loan at any time if the property is sold in this manner. It is at the lending institution's discretion whether to call the loan in case of violation of the due-on-sale clause. Some lenders may not call the loan if the payments due are made on time and there is no default. If the lender calls the loan and the buyer is unable to pay it off, then the lender may exercise the right to foreclose. The risk lies with the buyer.

In case of a loan assumption, the buyer assumes the loan after obtaining formal permission from the lender (or lending institution). Here the seller's name is deleted from the loan records and the buyer becomes the new borrower, similar to other purchase money loans. Usually, lenders charge the borrower an assumption fee for processing such a loan assumption. However, this fee is far lower than that for obtaining a conventional loan. Most conventional loans do not permit loan assumption.

SECONDARY MORTGAGE MARKET

On reading this section completely, you will understand;

- What are the key differences between Primary and Secondary mortgage markets?
- What is Fannie Mae and its significance?
- What is Freddie Mac and its link to mortgage markets?
- What is Ginnie Mae and how is it different from the other two?

PRIMARY VS SECONDARY MARKET

Primary mortgage market is the market where the loan originators and borrowers group together to negotiate interest rates, contract terms and finalize mortgage transactions. Banks, financial institutions, mortgage bankers, credit unions and mortgage brokers are all components of the primary mortgage market.

After originating in the primary mortgage market, majority of the mortgages are offered for sale in the secondary mortgage market. Many borrowers are ignorant of the fact that their mortgages become parts of combined / bulk mortgage packages that include mortgage-backed security (MBS), collateralized mortgage obligation (CMO) or asset-backed security (ABS) that are eventually sold to investors like pension funds, hedge funds and insurance companies, which form the secondary mortgage market. Mortgage-backed securities are commonly integrated into collateralized debt obligations (CDO) that encase other debt obligations like corporate loans.

The secondary mortgage market was created to serve as a new source of capital for the mortgage market to supplement the traditional source such as 'thrifts' proved inadequate to support it. This new source was expected to have greater efficiency compared to the older localized market which may experience shortage or surplus of funds according to its location. This aggregation process significantly reduced the risk of default concerning individual loans to an extent that made it feasible to treat high-risk individual loans as AAA-risk (safest level) investments.

FANNIE MAE - FNMA - FEDERAL NATIONAL MORTGAGE ASSOCIATION

The Federal National Mortgage Association (FNMA), popularly known as Fannie Mae, was formed in 1938 by amending the National Housing Act. It is a government-sponsored enterprise (GSE), despite being a publicly traded entity since 1968. It was established for offering federal money to local banks for financing home mortgages with the intent of enhancing home ownership levels and making affordable housing accessible. It spawned a liquid secondary mortgage market, enabling banks and various loan originators to disburse more housing loans, mainly through purchase of insured mortgages from the Federal Housing Association (FHA).

In 1950, Fannie Mae was acquired from the Federal Loan Agency by the Housing and Home Finance Agency and included as its constituent unit. In 1954, the passing of the Federal National Mortgage Association Charter Act transformed Fannie Mae into a 'mixed ownership corporation' with the federal government holding the preferred stock and private investors holding the common stock.

In 1968, it was changed to a privately-held corporation to exclude its debt and activities from the federal budget. With the passing of the Housing and Urban Development Act of 1968, the original Fannie Mae was bifurcated in to the present version of Fannie Mae and Ginnie Mae (Government National Mortgage Association).

Freddie Mac generates revenues and profits partially from borrowings at low rates and reinvesting into whole mortgages and mortgaged-backed securities (MBS). It sells bonds in the debt market to borrow funds and offers liquidity to mortgage originators by buying whole loans, securitizing them and producing MBS for retention or sale. The law mandates it to offer liquidity in all economic conditions to mortgage originators.

A significant part of its income is generated through guaranty fees received as compensation for taking on the credit risk associated with mortgage loans underlying its single-family MBS and those in its retained portfolio.

In 1970, the federal government permitted Fannie Mae to buy private mortgages (not insured by FHA, VA or FmHA) and established the Federal Home Loan Mortgage Corporation (FHMLC), popularly called 'Freddie Mac'. Its purpose was to generate healthy competition in the secondary mortgage market and make it stronger and more efficient. It is also a government-sponsored enterprise and like other GSEs it buys mortgages on sale in the secondary market, groups them together and offers them for sale as mortgage-backed securities in the open market. The secondary market raises the supply of money meant for mortgage lending as well as for new home purchases.

Freddie Mac generates revenues and profits primarily by charging a guarantee fee on the loans that it purchases and securitizes into mortgage-backed security (MBS) bonds. Investors and purchasers of such MBS allow Freddie Mac to retain the fee for taking on the credit risk, which involves issuing a guarantee about repayment of the principal and interest applicable on the underlying loan, irrespective of the borrower actually repaying or defaulting on it. This guarantee makes these MBS specifically attractive to investors.

GINNIE MAE - GNMA - GOVERNMENT 'NATIONAL MORTGAGE ASSOCIATION

The Government National Mortgage Association (GNMA), popularly called 'Ginnie Mae', was setup in 1968 to encourage home ownership in the United States. It is a wholly-owned government corporation and not a GSE like Fannie Mae or Freddie Mac. Its goal is to foster affordable housing by redirecting global capital into the housing finance markets in the U.S.A.

It guarantees on-time payment of principal and interest applicable on residential MBS to global institutional investors. MBS are known as 'pass through' certificates as the principal and interest linked to underlying loans are 'passed through' to those investing in them. These securities or repositories of mortgage loans serve as collateral for issuing securities on Wall Street.

The Ginnie Mae guarantee enables mortgage lenders to negotiate a better pricing for their loans in the stock markets. Then, lenders can channelize the proceeds to issue new mortgage loans to consumers. This lowers financing costs and generates opportunities for sustainable, affordable homes for families aspiring for home ownership.

Ginnie Mae guarantees only such securities that are supported by single-family and multifamily loans which are insured by government agencies such as FHA, VA and HUD etc. It neither originates nor buys mortgage loans and also does not buy, sell or issue securities. It neither uses derivatives to hedge nor carries long-term debt on its balance sheet. Private lenders approved by Ginnie Mae originate qualified loans, group them into securities and give out Ginnie Mae MBS. These institutions could be mortgage companies, thrifts of varying sizes, commercial banks and state housing finance companies.

Ginnie Mae is the exclusive home-loan agency which is explicitly reinforced by the 'full faith and credit' guarantee of the government of the United States.

TRUTH - IN LENDING - REGULATION Z

(15 U.S.C. § 1635 and 12 C.F.R. § 226.23)

On reading this section completely, you will understand;

- What is the Truth-in-Lending Act (TILA) or Regulation Z?
- What businesses are covered under its purview?
- What are the mandatory disclosures under TILA?
- What is the 'right of rescission' under TILA and when does it apply?
- What are the advertising regulations specified by TILA?

COVERAGE - BUSINESSES

The Truth-in-Lending Act (TILA), also known as 'Regulation Z', was enacted with the intention of enabling customers to differentiate between the costs involved in cash and credit transactions as well as the credit offered by different lenders.

In general, TILA applies to every individual or business, which offers credit, when,

➢ Such credit is extended to borrowers (consumers).

➢ A finance charge is applicable on such credit or if the credit is repayable in more than four installments as agreed in writing.

➢ The primary purpose of obtaining the credit is to use it for personal, family or household requirements.

➢ The loan balance is equal to or higher than $25000.

> ➤ The loan is secured by an interest in a residential or other real property, where such property covers 25 acres or more; or the property is vacant land meant for constructing a home within two years from settlement using the loan funds.

> ➤ The loan is a temporary loan backed by a real estate security (construction-only loan).

Mortgages not covered by TILA (as per new rules) are;

> ➤ Home Equity Lines of Credit (HELOC).

> ➤ Reverse mortgages.

> ➤ Loans secured by mobile homes or residences that are not attached to land.

> ➤ Loans offered by creditors extending five or lesser loans in a year.

DISCLOSURE

TILA regulations require all lenders to disclose certain details about loans offered as per the Real Estate Settlement Procedures Act (RESPA), within three business days after receiving a written application from a borrower. This is the early disclosure statement which is partly based on the information provided initially by the borrower (consumer). A final disclosure statement is given just before loan closing.

The disclosures have to be in a particular format and include the following details;

> ➤ Name and Address of the borrower (creditor)

> ➤ Amount of the loan applied for

> ➤ Itemized statement of the loan amount to be financed (not required if Good Faith Estimate is given)

> ➤ Annual Percentage Rate (APR)

> ➤ Variable rate, if applicable

> ➤ Finance charges

> ➤ Total number of payment installments

> ➤ Payment schedule

- Demand terms and conditions

- Total selling price

- Prepayment terms and conditions

- Late payment penalty and other terms

- Insurance requirements

- Security interest charges

- Specific security interest fees

- Assumption terms and conditions

- Deposits required

- Contract reference

ARM loans require additional disclosures if the annual percentage rate on the loan that is secured by the borrower's primary home increases after consummation and the loan term is more than one year. These are;

- A copy of the Consumer Handbook on Adjustable Rate Mortgage, that is published by the Federal Home Loan Bank Board or an equivalent body.

- A disclosure about the loan details of each variable-rate loan that the borrower is interested in. Such a disclosure should include all essential information as stipulated by Regulation Z.

- TILA requires service providers to furnish subsequent disclosure to borrowers regarding variable-rate transactions in each such month when the interest rate was adjusted.

On November 20, 2013, the Consumer Finance Protection Board (CFPB), under authorization from the Dodd-Frank Act, unfurled the new rule that integrates the mortgage disclosures required under the Real Estate Settlement Procedures Act (RESPA) a.k.a. Regulation X and the Truth-in-Lending Act (TILA) a.k.a. Regulation Z. This new rule will be effective for applications received on or after August 1, 2015.

This new rule is republished in Chapter X of C.F.R. Title 12.

RIGHT OF RESCISSION

Under the Truth-in-Lending Act, the 'right of rescission' is practically a 'right to cancel' a mortgage transaction and claim refund of any fees paid, if the borrower is dissatisfied with the loan for any particular reason(s). The right to rescind is essentially a time period provided to homeowners opting for refinancing their mortgage, to think things over clearly prior to committing to the new mortgage terms.

After receiving a mortgage refinance approval and signing the new loan documents, the borrower acquires the right to rescind over the subsequent three business days. The borrower may regret the decision to refinance which may have been triggered due to pressure from a mortgage broker or bank or being victimized by predatory lending and want to back out of the transaction. Hence the right to rescission provision is made in the Truth-in-Lending Act. It is a mechanism to protect the consumer (borrower).

Rescission Period = Time to Change the Decision. During this period the borrower gets the opportunity to mull over the situation and decide clearly whether to go ahead or back out of the transaction. The borrower may change their mind during the three days rescission period and without attracting any penalty.

The rescission period starts at midnight, the day after signing of the loan documents and ends after three subsequent business days including Saturdays, but excluding Sundays and federal holidays. The rescission periods end at midnight of the third business day and the loan documents signed are treated as 'official' thereafter.

In case of rescission of the mortgage, all the fees are required to be refunded to the borrower. These include lender's fees such as application and processing fees etc.; broker fees; and fees paid to third parties such as title and appraisal fees, either directly or through the lender. Fees paid by the borrower to a third party outside the credit transaction, including building and zoning permit fees, are non-refundable.

The borrower has to issue a written notice of rescission of the mortgage to the lender during the rescission period. The lender must then take necessary action to terminate the transaction such as canceling the loan documents, filing the release statements in public records and refunding the relevant fees to the borrower. The lender has to complete all these activities within 20 calendar days from the receipt of the rescission notice.

Right of rescission is restricted to refinancing of owner-occupied properties only.

In case of direct advertisement by a lender to a consumer, TILA mandates that such an advertisement should disclose the credit terms and interest rate in a specific manner. If a credit advertisement mentions specific credit terms, it should mention only such terms that are or will be actually offered or arranged by the lender. If an advertisement mentions a rate of finance charges, it should be presented in the form of an 'annual percentage rate' (APR). If the APR increases after consummation the advertisement should mention that fact. The advertisement should not mention any other rate with the exception of a simple annual or periodic rate along with, but not with greater highlight than, the annual percentage rate.

MORTGAGE NOTE AND MORTGAGE DEED

On reading this section completely, you will understand;

- What is a Grantor / Grantee Deed?
- What is a Mortgagor / Mortgagee Deed?
- What is a Mortgage Note?

GRANTOR/GRANTEE DEED

(M.G.L. c. 183A)

A Deed is a legal document that conveys ownership of real property interests from one party to another. A deed is usually a short document, but embodies the entire purpose for the underlying transaction (i.e. transfer of real property) and this makes it a vital component of every property purchase and sale transaction. In a deed, usually the party conveying the real property is called the 'grantor' (or seller) and the party receiving the real property is called the 'grantee' (or buyer).

The deed document includes details about the seller (grantor), the buyer (grantee), the method of taking title to the property (tenancy) by the grantee, the consideration (amount of the purchase price), the property's legal description and a citation to the registry records of the previous deed. The grantee also wants to include specific covenants of title or assurances that the grantor holds a good and marketable title to the property, possesses the right to convey the property and the property is free and clear of any undisclosed encumbrances. On signing of the deed document by the parties involved, it is recorded at the recorder's office in the local county where the property is physically located. The deed is usually drafted by the attorney of the Seller.

(M.G.L. c. 183. § 18)

The mortgage deed is a legal document that offers security interest in a real estate to a mortgage lender. A borrower pledges his or her property as security to obtain a loan and the deed denotes the ownership rights of the lender in the pledged real estate. The borrower of the loan is called the 'mortgagor' and the lender who offers the loan against ownership and foreclosure rights on the property is called the 'mortgagee' (M.G.L. c. 244. § 35A).

The mortgage deed bestows on the lender foreclosure rights to the property in the event that the borrower fails to fulfill the mortgage obligations. All mortgage lenders make borrowers sign a mortgage deed or trust deed at the time of signing of the promissory note (Mortgage note) and before actual disbursal of loan funds. In Massachusetts, the mortgage lenders must use this document as a means for securing the home loans given out to the borrowers.

Mortgage Note (M.G.L. c. 183)

A mortgage note is a promise to repay a debt, which is secured by a mortgage, contract or trust deed. When appropriately drafted, such a note can be sold to generate immediate cash. It is common practice to accept a trust deed or mortgage in the form of a note as a part of a property sale proceeds.

OTHER BOOKS:

Massachusetts Real Estate: An Instructor Preparation Course

Massachusetts Real Estate Broker - Book I

Massachusetts Real Estate Broker - Book II

Real Estate Math: Sample Problems and Solutions

Massachusetts Real Estate Salesperson - Book I

Massachusetts Real Estate Salesperson - Book II

How to increase sales using YouTube

How to increase sales using Pinterest

How to increase sales using Facebook

BUSINESSES SERVICES:

Innovative Publishers Inc.

http://innovative-publishers.com

Innovative Publishers is a broad-based publisher with experience in literary and commercial fiction, business books, children's books, cookbooks, mystery, romance, reference, religious and spiritual books. Find new book releases, best sellers lists and see when your favorite Innovative Publishers author is making their next appearance. Innovative Publishers in your place for novels and new books

---

Taylor Pam Fine Homes & Investment

http://tpfh-ma.com/

A boutique real estate agency in Back Bay. Taylor Pam Fine Homes & Investment (TPFH) is committed to delivering a high level of expertise, customer service, and attention to detail to the marketing and sales of luxury real estate, new developments, and vacation and rental properties.

Global Realty & Investment Corp

http://gric-ma.com/
Facebook: https://www.facebook.com/globalrealtyinvestment
Twitter: @GRIC_MA
Pinterest: http://pinterest.com/gricma/

Offers real estate services and working capital loans

Taylor Pam - Fine Artist - Photographer – Designer
http://taylorpam.com

Taylor Pam is a Boston based contemporary artist offering abstract paints, portraits, private commissions and prints.

Premier Development
https://www.facebook.com/pages/Premier-Development/

Full service construction company serving eastern Massachusetts. Offers full service construction services. Remodeling, flooring and landscaping.

Intergalactic Travel Authority
http://ita-travelauthority.com/
http://www.pinterest.com/itatravel/
https://twitter.com/intergalacticTA

GROUPGLOBAL.NET

https://www.facebook.com/cybershoptoday

Online shopping for books, magazines, music, DVDs, videos, electronics, computers, software, apparel, accessories, shoes, jewelry, tools, hardware, housewares, furniture, sporting goods, beauty, personal care, and much more. Corporate branding and office supplies.

ABOUT THE AUTHOR

Ms. Claretta T. Pam is the lead instructor at the Boston School of Real Estate Inc., a business professor at Oplerno.com, and is an Adjunct Professor at Bunker Hill Community College, Charlestown, Massachusetts, USA. Ms. Pam is a construction supervisor and licensed home improvement contractor in Massachusetts. She was educated at the University of Massachusetts Boston in Boston, MA, USA and graduated with Bachelors degrees in Political Science and Studio Art. She earned a Masters in Business Administration with a concentration in eCommerce from the University of Phoenix, USA. She is the managing director at Global Realty & Investment Corp and Taylor Pam Fine Homes & Investment in Boston, MA.